# MUSIC
# POWER
# HARMONY

# MUSIC
# POWER
# HARMONY
## A Workbook of Music and Inner Forces

## R. J. Stewart

BLANDFORD

Blandford
An imprint of Cassell
Villiers House, 41–47 The Strand, London WC2

First published 1990

Distributed in the United States by
Sterling Publishing Co, Inc,
387 Park Avenue South, New York, NY 10016–8810

Distributed in Australia by
Capricorn Link (Australia) Pty Ltd
PO Box 665, Lane Cove, NSW 2066

**British Library Cataloguing in Publication Data**
Stewart, R. J. (Robert J), 1949–
    Music power harmony: a workbook of music and inner
    forces.
    1. Music. Psychological aspects
    I. Title
    781.11

    ISBN 0–7137—2121–9

Set in 10/12 Sabon by Butler & Tanner Ltd, Frome and London
Printed and bound in Great Britain by
Biddles Ltd., Guildford and King's Lynn

# Contents

List of Illustrations  ·  6
How to Use this Book  ·  7
Introduction  ·  11

1   Music and Collective Consciousness  ·  19
2   Ancient Temple Music  ·  27
3   Harmonics and Hierarchies  ·  35
4   Images and Inspiration  ·  41
5   Invoking Apollo  ·  49
6   Therapy, Emotions, Patterns  ·  61
7   Hearing Beyond Hearing  ·  65
8   Squares, Sigils, Sacred Dance  ·  71
9   Voices From the Void:
     Cosmology, Music, the Tree of Life  ·  79
10  Music, Tarot, the Axis Mundi  ·  97
11  Crystals, Time, Stars  ·  109
12  Vowels, Breath, Energy  ·  117
13  Colour, Scales, Music  ·  133
14  Elemental Calls in Three Worlds:
     A training programme  ·  141

Appendix 1:   Music from the Ancestors  ·  157
Appendix 2:   Synthesizers and Computers  ·  162
Appendix 3:   Plato's *Myth of Er*  ·  167
Appendix 4:   *Apollo and Orpheus,
     Their Myths and Symbols* (William King, 1710)  ·  172

Bibliography  ·  186
Index  ·  188

# List of Illustrations

Figure 1    The Four Elements    ·    30

Figure 2    The Spiral of Octaves    ·    36

Figure 3    The Planetary Lyre    ·    54

Figure 4    The Four Energy Centres and Four Elements    ·    74

Figure 5    The Tree of Life    ·    86

Figure 6    The Axis Mundi and Tarot Images    ·    102

Figure 7    Breathing the Six Directions    ·    120

Figure 8    Vowels Chants and Elements    ·    126

Figure 9    The Lunar Solar and Stellar Modes    ·    148

# How to Use this Book

This book aims to combine several methods of inner transformation which I have examined, discussed, and developed for modern use in earlier works. The emphasis here, however, is solely upon music as a means to inner liberation. In some of the practical exercises it expands upon my earlier book *Music and the Elemental Psyche*,[1] but it is independent from it, and written to be used without detailed cross-reference to its predecessor. This is not a book which follows the now well-trodden path of listing recordings and styles of music and suggesting a programme of listening and associated meditation or self-affirmation: there is no progressive discography or recommended listening list.

At the risk of drawing howls of wrath from some writers, musicians, and music enthusiasts, I would suggest that such methods are of little use in the context of permanent transformation and empowerment through music. Our technological culture is remarkably passive ... how might we use music for inner growth if, terrible thought, the electricity failed? We need to seek deeper within consciousness to find the source of musical empowerment, and I feel that this is best represented by the pervasive Elemental world-view, in which a fourfold cycle of relative energies is employed to define and transform all conditions, from atomic to psychic to universal. Genetics uses an Elemental system, having discovered that the organic life code is based upon a fourfold spiral; but this simple universal fact was and still is taught in the enduring inner and outer schools of spiritual development. The Elemental system is not a quaint pre-scientific or redundant subject; but we do have to be cautious and seek perpetually to work with it in a manner suitable for our own time and place.

Chapters 1–7 deal with a general theory of music and musical traditions concerning consciousness and empowerment, while Chapters 8–14 give a working example of a system of Elemental Chant, which may also be adapted for instrumental music. This system is within the holistic traditions of meditation and music found worldwide, but there is no requirement of the student that he or she become deeply absorbed into specific schools of metaphysics or mysticism. I would suggest that, having read the general theory and discussion of music and consciousness, simple practical experimentation with the *Elemental Calls* will do far more than endless further reading.

For those who wish a more visually orientated type of exercise, I have included a guided visualization (see Chapter 5), which uses traditional imagery assembled and restated in a manner designed to bring the modern consciousness into contact with primal energies concerned with music and the relationship of music to living entities. It sounds complex, but it really is nothing more than vivid storytelling under meditative circumstances. Balance comes, of course, by combining the visual and auditory methods of musical empowerment, though the emphasis is always upon sound.

This is intended as a modern workbook, not an academic exercise in musical history. It discusses topics that range from the metaphysical music of the Ancient Greeks to the influence of lysergic acid upon popular music in the twentieth century. The emphasis is always upon the practical: how we can use music, tones, pitches, sounds, to empower our inner development? As a result of this some of the increasingly obvious negative aspects of modern culture and its mass-music are also examined.

There is no need for the reader to be a musician or a composer or a psychologist, though specialists in any creative or psychic art or discipline should find interesting material that touches upon their own field of work. You can use this book, and the techniques for visualization and chanting or playing elemental patterns upon instruments, even if you have no experience in such matters.

It is not, however, a beginners' book in meditation or mystical and magical arts; areas that are repeatedly published, such as the power of the imagination, the effects of the will, benefits of meditation, and so forth are taken as established facts that need not have time or space wasted further upon them.

Technical jargon is kept to an absolute minimum throughout: very few references are made to specialist musical terminology, and no mathematical theorems or cross-references to technical works are employed. There are, however, a small number of references in the text that relate to the Bibliography, where books for further study are listed; a number of these deal in depth with technical matters concerning music, physics, mathematics, cosmology, and many of the subjects which are becoming increasingly related to one another as holisms are rediscovered by modern science.

Rediscovery is, in many ways, the keynote of this book. It does not offer tedious discussions of how the ancients might or might not have used certain scales, or the calculation of planetary orbits by musical patterns and proportions prior to the telescope, or any of the scientific or historical material that might be used in an intellectual survey of music and consciousness. Instead several related holistic traditions are described, and a direct practical method of applying music to these is offered. The concepts and perceptions (world-view) are of far greater importance than nit-picking over rates of vibration; music works through proportions, and proportions apply to any set of numbers, regardless of their detailed content.

The term *tradition* appears frequently in the following chapters, and I am aware that a valid accusation might be levelled that this and similar books repeatedly hark back to a mysterious but essentially unknowable past. The justification for this reference to ancient tradition is really one of experience: the perennial traditions offer little in the way of hard facts as required by material science, but a great deal in the way of insight and technique for expanding consciousness. The traditional concepts of holism, universal entity, harmonic relationship between life forms and other matters discussed more fully later, can no longer be dismissed as idle superstition. Modern research into physics, genetics, holography, and other 'new' sciences repeatedly establishes that ancient concepts of holism, of unification and harmony through proportional relationships, abound in the universe.

There is no point in advocating ancient tradition merely as a conservative or romantic source of obscurity or escape: anyone truly delving into the perennial arts of spiritual or inner transformation will find that they are strict, demanding, and potent.

So to use this book I would suggest that you read through the entire text without attempting any practical examples. Next I would propose that most readers will be initially drawn to one of the two basic techniques offered, guided visualization or Elemental Chanting. Work with the one that is initially most appealing, but try both. The exercises for Elemental tones, breathing, dedicating Sacred Space, and related subjects are designed to be carried over a cycle of one year, but it is also possible to work within other proportional time cycles. Thus each stage could be worked in one day initially, or for one week, or one month. As long as the proportions are constant, the timescale is really a matter of your own preference and dedication. Do not expect immediate 'results' . . . if you do have experiences that hit you like falling thunderbolts as a result of this or any similar technique, you are probably deluding yourself, even though such effects do, very rarely, occur. Your own intuition is always the best guide and judge.

The greater amount of space and exposition in the last seven chapters is dedicated to Elemental patterns and calls; but they may then be used with some of the associated traditions of inner development, such as the Tree of Life or the Tarot. I would hasten to add that these systems are not approached from an 'occult' viewpoint, but as holistic universal models of energy and consciousness; occultism plays little or no part in such matters, and I would predict that within the next century terms such as 'occult' and all the trivial juvenile nonsense associated with such terms will have vanished altogether from the vocabulary of inner growth or spiritual development.

R. J. Stewart, Bath.

# Introduction

## Chaos Sounds Fullness

There are two ways to apprehend music. The first is that selected sounds fill emptiness. This is the standard understanding of music, and is, indeed, the popularly accepted concept behind modern sciences, behind physics, behind many underlying assumptions and conceptual models deeply embedded in human culture and in Western civilization. In brief, the universe is seen as a void, as empty space, within which interactions of energy and physical objects appear. The why and wherefore of their appearance and interactions are the pursuit of physicists, and have been continually redefined during the last 200 years, with some radical changes during the twentieth century.

Music has long been used as a tuitional model for understanding the universe, with various experiments and expositions dating from as far back as Pythagoras to the work of Renaissance adepts such as Marcilio Ficino, Robert Fludd, or Athanasius Kircher, and of the great musical cosmologist and physicist Johannes Kepler, leading into the mathematics and physics of Newton. Such profound thinkers, philosophers, and practical metaphysicians all used musical experiments, actual definable and proven musical events and measurements, to reveal cosmological truths. This simply means that certain patterns and proportions occurring in nature, in acoustics, in physical movement of objects when set in motion, readily demonstrable to anyone, are actual reflections (not analogies or similarities or metaphors, but direct reflections) of what appear to be cosmic patterns or 'laws'.

It is generally assumed that the 'emptiness-being-filled' model underpins this venerable tradition of music and physics, but such an assumption may be challenged. Before considering alternatives, however, we should pursue the emptiness-being-filled model in some detail, for it reveals a great deal to us.

In this first way, or conceptual mode, of apprehending music, the emptiness which is filled is both spatial, temporal, and acoustic (i.e. sounds fill silence). The spatial quality is clearly expressed in abstract in the notation of music, where spatial proportions act as analogies of temporal rhythmic and pitched notes. More simply, we see abstract lines of dots rising and falling over a graph, the lines of the musical stave. Thus musical concepts and patterns are giving a spatial 'two-dimensional' analogy which may be retranslated to re-create music.

In Western art music, the score is usually identical in the minds of musician, composer, or even audience with the actual music. Thus the music of an individual composer is not regarded as the sound-picture made by a performance, but as the notation upon paper. This concept gives us considerable insight into the collective and historical development of Western consciousness since the Middle Ages, during the latter part of which music was first written out.

The spatial quality, in our first mode of apprehension 'emptiness-being-filled', is also apparent in acoustics, in physics. A musical note, or a sequence, or an entire symphony is emitted initially from a specific location (a single instrument, voice, or the multiple combinations thereof with larger musical forces) and travels through the medium of air as a series of vibrations or waves. These gradually decrease in effect over a distance, until they are beyond human hearing, as their physical energy has been, so to speak, expended.

This second spatial quality is linked to that of time: not only do the notes of the music, the patterns played and heard, fit a certain external time complex of durations and rhythms, but the passage of the sounds through air, through locatable directions of space, takes a certain measurable time: the speed of sound. But this is merely the surface of the soundscape, for within even a single uttered tone, be it vocal or instrumental, there are inherent a large number of overtones or partials: these have their own durations, their own life, and many complete sequences of interaction within and between themselves. Thus any musical performance, even the simplest melody, has many timescales and spatial thresholds within it.

We need consider all of the foregoing only briefly to realize that once we follow through the emptiness-being-filled model, it reduces itself, or perhaps expands itself, to absurdity. There is no clearly defined temporal or spatial restriction or pattern to a piece of music: all such thresholds are relative.

Before music begins there is silence; but that silence itself is full of sounds. When the music commences, it generates patterns that resonate through the (non-) silence that preceded it, but each fragment of the music holds countless moments of resonance, interaction, silence, and sound. The standard conceptual model of music, as something which is generated to fill silence according to predefined patterns, or in the case of a score, according to a map, is insufficient.

This leads us to the second mode of apprehending music, which is that it consists of patterns temporarily defined out of a *pleroma*, a fullness of other patterns. Physically this is more accurate, and corresponds to the most advanced theories and experiments of modern science. There is no physical emptiness, no hollow of space into which music, or indeed matter, suddenly appears. There is fullness within which certain patterns appear and reiterate as harmonic entities of one another. Music proves this.

Thus when Pythagoras, in Ancient Greece, measured a stretched string or wire, and taught its mystical and physical proportions in relationship to pitch and the musical scale, he was not attempting the first experiment in materialist physics. He was revealing that nature mirrors the universe, and that proportions and patterns are inherent in all matter due to polarity and interaction. More subtly, he was causing a physical sound to resonate through the human consciousness and body, and so by harmonics stimulating certain proportions and patterns of energy in that human entity. The sets of proportions or laws deduced from this magical experiment acted in various forms as foundations for all ancient civilization, and continued through into Renaissance and Hermetic arts and sciences. But modern science (derived from the magical arts, though most unwilling to admit it) took the letter of experimentation to extremes and abandoned its musical spirit, by which higher octaves of any relationship are always present during an event.

The old Hermetic axiom, 'As above so below', the concept of a human microcosm reflecting the universal macrocosm – these are essentially musical statements. Anyone who has heard an octave sound, by which we can probably include every person on the planet who has average hearing abilities, many people even with limited hearing, and even some totally deaf people who can still perceive ratios and proportions in physical vibrations through the body, can perceive for themselves the law of 'As above so below'.

In this book we shall be exploring a range of the less-perceived harmonies, patterns, and empowering uses of music. It is not a musical textbook, and as far as possible musical technical language has been carefully excluded. It is specifically aimed at assisting the individual or group wishing to use music for inner transformation.

## Where is Silence?

Where is silence? It clearly is not in the relative reduction of sound or lessening of random noise prior to an utterance of music. This relative silence is so full of sound that it is deafening: if you doubt this, simply consider a concert hall in that tense, expectant moment before the performers strike the first note ... or consider yourself, alone in a room, before you open your mouth to utter a vowel or a chant. Is there silence? Even in the single body, sitting alone in a soundproof chamber, there is a rushing torrent of sound from the breath, the blood, the organs. The presumably still air in the room is continually moving and making its own sound, stirred by your breath, by the wind from beneath the door, by the tiny vibrations emitted by the walls as they respond to energies impinging from outside the building.

Silence is uniquely found through our consciousness: it is within.

## Empowering through Music

One of the aims of this book is to discuss and propose methods by which we might empower ourselves through music. 'Empowering' has becoming a fashionable term in recent years, often applied frivolously, and may for many of us have negative connotations, such as gaining ascendancy over unsuspecting or unwilling people. Before proceeding to methods, therefore, we need to examine concepts of empowerment, and of music power. Indeed, without a proper grasp of key concepts, the techniques and traditions of empowerment, which may be realized through a number of different vehicles, of which music is one of the most potent, cannot be understood and cannot be fully applied for practical purposes.

The *Oxford English Dictionary* defines 'empower' as follows: 'to impart power (to do something), to enable, to permit'. The dictionary also gives a legal definition of empowerment, by which legal right and power is granted to take certain actions or act with specific authority; this might seem less important in our present context, but it has subtle implications to which we shall return shortly in terms of music, power, and harmony.

Empowering through music enables us to do something, something which we otherwise might not be able to undertake. The musical empowerment enables us *to permit* ourselves, to give ourselves permission, to be transformed. Thus the empowering is effective upon ourselves, rather than used for, or squandered upon, gaining illusory control or power over others.

This inner permission and application has an analogy to that legal definition found in the dictionary, for the legitimate use of power is always towards transformation, rather than towards retention and stagnation. This is, of course, contentious ground for philosophical and political discussion, but we are not concerned here with politics or materialist dialectic. The types of power, transformation, and legitimization under discussion are all inner, creative, imaginative, bioelectrical events, acting upon an individual or a group, and even on national or international collective levels.

Note that the term *psychological* is not automatically included in our definition of inner transformation, though the psychological effect of music is undeniable, provided we adhere to a psychological model or definition of humanity.

Musical empowerment, however, comes from well-established and enduring traditions which predate modern psychology by many centuries, often by millennia. Such traditions have a detailed, refined and effective magical or esoteric psychology of their own, which, like other spiritual traditions of our world, makes modern materialist studies of the human psyche pale into insignificance.

But why are certain actions, changes, inner forces or empowerments legitimate while others are not? The laws referred to are not the statutes or decisions of politics or dogmatic political religions, nor are they derived from any of the limited and regularly outmoded sets of laws posited by materialist science; they are patterns inherent within the universe. It is at this universal level that modern science, particularly physics, has turned full circle and joined (albeit unconsciously or unwillingly) with the perennial spiritual or metaphysical traditions.

Certain 'laws' may be said to apply to the generation and transformation of energy within the human being. These laws are reflections, or, in musical terms, *harmonics*, of universal patterns. What appears to be a law, what seems at first an insurmountable barrier, either for the individual seeking inner liberation or for humanity, is merely a reflection, a harmonic, of a reiterating pattern in universal terms, and is never immutable, rigid, or eternal. Terms such as immutable, eternal, divine law, and similar dogmatic phrases have some very negative connotations indeed in modern society: they are seen, with considerable justification, as tools of suppression. If we adopt the understanding, the realization, that the universe is a *pleroma*, a fullness, in which nodes of energy appear, resonate, and disappear, then the potency of universal patterns remains, and the dogmatic possibility of restrictive laws vanishes.

The entire customary mental structure of 'laws' in science, by which laws had to be found, used, surmounted, defined, or exploited, has led to our current perilous planetary situation. Through so-called laws, an essentially antagonistic, divisive technology has developed by which humanity applies scientific knowledge to subvert or triumph over the apparent laws of nature. We are now realizing that this fantasy, this demonic destructive application of preconceived 'laws' towards short-term gain, acts only upon and against ourselves. We and the planet are one; abuse the land, the sea, the world, and we abuse ourselves. Once again, modern physics has belatedly discovered a truth which has long been taught openly and freely in esoteric tradition: the observer and the experiment are one; there is no infinite repetition, only harmonic transformation.

Yet quite detailed sets of harmonic patterns have been known since ancient times, sometimes expressed poetically and mythically, and at other times in precise mathematical terms. The discoveries and laws of our materialist sciences are not true laws or patterns, but devolved subsets, distorted images, that seemed, for a little while, to give answers and provide benefits. The ultimate end of this distortion is, as we all know now, the fission of the atom. If we can destroy something, the false reasoning runs, we are able to control it. But what we destroy is ourselves.

True empowerment enables us to permit, to attune, to harmonize. What we attune to, harmonize with, is not any vague spiritualized set of beliefs or carefully assembled code of ethics, but the universe itself. At one time this might have been regarded as an impossible statement to prove, the product of wild mysticism or outmoded superstition. But, as the ancient philosophers and metaphysicians maintained, and as the esoteric traditions have taught in both East and West in an unbroken stream of instruction from primal culture to the present day, the individual and the universe resonate within one another.

Modern physics confirms this with theories and models in which it is clear that the observer and the experiment interact upon one another; this interaction is applicable and true through to a universal level.

Empowerment through music, therefore, must employ resonances, patterns, harmonics, that are inherent within the universe. But surely all patterns generated are, obviously, inherent within the universe? This is where modern scientific disciplines, particularly the new advances in sciences such as physics, genetics, and holography, begin to meet with the esoteric traditions. Certain resonances, shapes, frequencies, or qualities of event are ubiquitous. They appear as harmonics of one another throughout the fields of being, existence, creation. Other resonances or events are temporary, comparatively limited, and contained within time, confined to a narrower range, and often maintained only through unnatural devices or supporting technologies.

There are many analogies in modern sciences to this type of situation, but as it is one of energy, the world fuel and energy crisis springs immediately to mind. There are potent universal, solar, and planetary energies. Elemental forces such as wind and water, solar heat and light, are all well within our grasp and technical abilities to utilize to generate applicable energy for domestic and industrial use. Modern studies have shown repeatedly that such energy sources can be relatively cheaply utilized and are non-destructive to the environment. By comparison we have the outdated and absurd processes of burning energy-rich fuels in order to generate electricity, or using nuclear fission to generate electricity.

Both of the last methods of energy production are examples of artificial constructs which cost (both financially and ecologically) far more than the value of the product which they produce; the situation, the event of energy generation, is artificial. It applies the limited unnatural 'laws' of chemistry and physics, as defined in the last century, in an unavoidably divisive, wasteful manner. The laws are limited, even warped, subsets of universal patterns, leading to waste, pollution, harmful radiation, potential planetary destruction. Yet we use them rather than harness other energy sources which are inherent within the planet's own pattern, life cycle, and energy field.

This analogy may be applied to music: the viewpont that any music is valid, that artistic statement outweighs all other factors, or conversely that what the public wants is what will always appear in commercial music, is strikingly similar to the energy-generating trap. What we gain, the end result, is far less valuable than the initial input, the concept or process of musical creation: the effects are often destructive, deadening, corrupting, and potentially deadly.

To explore this strange situation further, we need only remember that we constantly employ technology as a crude defence against natural resonance; our noise-generating devices, such as radio, television, and tape and disc players, our communications technology, using many artificial frequencies, all create a web, a cocoon, by which we close out whatever is truly present in our environment, our land, our planet, our solar system.

So there are patterns that are unnatural, forced, falsely maintained at great cost; these patterns involve energy. To find empowerment through music, we must first grasp the hard truth of our cocoon, our shell, our prison. Then we must give ourselves permission to step outside it, and hear, perhaps for the first time, what is happening in the great world of the universe. Paradoxically this stepping outside our shell, our cocoon of habit, electronic frequencies, devices, conditioning, pollution, miseducation, involves going within ourselves, in meditation, visualization, and intuitional arts and disciplines. These techniques are so well publicized and diversely taught today that they need no introduction here.

But having crossed that threshold and started meditating, there are some less well-known methods of realigning inner consciousness, the imagination, the emotions, the mental processes, the vital energies, and the physical body. These methods were once widely taught, if we are to accept esoteric tradition, and are now slowly being restated upon a new level, a new turn of the spiral of development, for the present day. The empowering effects of music are a major part of such holistic arts, offering us techniques in which physical utterances of audible sound have a potent effect upon our awareness, our energy levels, and our relationship to our local, planetary, and universal environment.

# 1 Music and Collective Consciousness

If we approach music historically, as an outer sign of changes of collective consciousness, a definition which it certainly fills in terms of both political and social history and of artistic expression, we may apply a generally historical thesis to consider the implications of present-day music. More simply, the true music of any period is its collective music, the musical vehicle for the majority of people: it speaks (or should speak) with their voice. In earlier centuries, and in less technologically orientated cultures, this definition was relatively easy to make, but in Western culture it is now increasingly hard to define where a collective or fundamental music may be found. Many people assert that this confused state is the beginning of a new musical awareness. This may be so, but it has not yet reached any level at which it may be recognized or defined: in short, it has not appeared yet.

Commercial recordings that claim in a grandiose manner to be the music of the New Age are often disappointing; besides, when the new age of musical awareness permeates through us all, it will need no labels or glossy covers, for we will all be aware of it as our own music. So collective music, the mass music of ordinary people, which was at one time strictly environmental, ethnic, or regional, no longer seems to permeate collective consciousness, for collective musical consciousness is in a state of flux, imbalance, and confusion.

Art music, by comparison, acts upon a very limited but often important level of consciousness, being communicated only to a tiny minority of the population. As the formalized creation of highly trained and creative or sensitive individuals, certain types of art music may be vehicles for those characteristic peaks of human consciousness available at, and typical to, certain phases of cultural development.

The mass media have not done a great deal to change the exclusivity of current art music, but they have helped greatly to communicate and make available the art music of previous centuries to a widening audience. The collective consciousness is, in terms of art music, very conservative, so the great works of certain composers of previous centuries only now begin to have a general popularity. Such popularity exists within social groups (through mass media) that would seldom or never go to classical or modern music concerts. Furthermore, this general popularity of early classics, promulgated through records, tapes, and CDs, reaches types or classes of people who would never have been reached by the original composers in their own century, for they are not part of the system of privilege and patronage that generated a classical art music in Western culture. By comparison to popular music, however, this is still a small audience.

It is, however, difficult to define 'classes' today in an adequate manner: the old rigid, suppressive class system in the West has been radically changed, and in its place we find a new class system based upon money, technology, and material symbols of superiority. Behind this materialistic class system, the older structure of aristocracy, upper and middle classes, and the far larger working class, still exists in an attenuated form. The difference is that whereas in earlier centuries only the middle classes could move into a state of 'privilege' through material gain, this potential accumulation of status runs through all levels of society today. It is, of course, a false image, based upon advertising, subtle suppressive conditioning, and the illusion that material benefit can truly replace all other human values.

Cyril Scott, the Theosophist composer and writer on music, proposed in his book *Music*[2] that the works of certain great composers were not merely individual advances in art music relative to their generation or century, but that they powerfully *steered* the social development of their era, or of later eras in which they were taken up on a wide scale. Thus the formal and excessively structured music of Handel, written in the eighteenth century, actually generated the collective values of the Victorian middle class by exposing them to musical patterns which caused them to react both mentally and emotionally in certain rigid, formalized ways. Conversely, the modern music of composers such as Stravinsky and others working with complex rhythms, non-formal structures, and tonal experiments acted as a force to break up the rigid society of the West, a breaking which was manifested ultimately as the two world wars.

Obviously, I am summarizing Scott's thesis in a superficial manner, as it fundamentally depends upon certain Theosophical propositions, such as the existence of hidden 'Masters' who guide the development of humanity (and so are supposed to directly influence key composers). Most of this type of Theosophical esoteric theory seems unacceptable today, as it is so denigrating of the individual human spirit and potential for inner transformation. If we think that we can do nothing to realize our potential without the steering influence of the Masters, we are in terrible danger of spiritual apathy. Whether or not such Masters exist is, of course, another discussion altogether from that of their superhuman control of social and human evolution, such as was described at length, even ad nauseam, by Theosophists in the last century.

It seems to me that (setting aside the dogma of the Theosophical Society) though Scott's approach to art music has considerable insight, for it places the *creative forces* first in line of interpretation, and their individual mediators, the composers, and social manifestation second, it entirely ignores the musicality of the majority of the population. I do not intend to proceed with any criticism of Scott in particular, as his book is in many ways excellent, and was the first modern book of this sort to have any wide readership and effect. It is essential, though, to criticize and re-examine the curiously blinkered attitude of so many otherwise profound writers and thinkers involved in music; they limit themselves entirely to the very small field of activity of art music.

Meanwhile, the culture, the continent, the planet, all have immense musical traditions, interactions, and patterns, which reach millions and millions of people and are not part of art music at all. This simple fact of collective music was true before mass media, and though the world-picture is now complicated by mass media and greatly transformed, it still holds good in cultures and places maintaining an ethnic or collective music inheritance that owes little to art, patronage, or individual creative genius. The current attention being paid to 'World Music', often ruthlessly promoted as nothing more nor less than an alternative pop product, indicates that people's intuitive and inner need for music with environmental and collective roots is not being satisfied. Environmental music is not a quaint folksy relic to be trotted out on public holidays or on obscure small record company releases, but a living fact of human energy and consciousness. It is the result of our Elemental life forces interacting with the land, the continent, the planet. Our ultimate environment is not only this planet, Earth, but our solar system and the universe beyond.

So Westerners, rebelling against the avaricious and dehumanized product of the pop video, find resonances within the primal and classical musics of the East, and more recently of Africa. Ironically, these world musics have much in common with the ethnic musics of the West, which have been virtually wiped out during the twentieth century.

Nor should this proposition be surprising: fundamental ethnic or collective musics derive from the interaction between people and their land: the music consciousness, the music power, is shared by us all, while the specific geographical environments shape its localized or national expression.

In earlier centuries the musical picture was relatively simple: a small privileged minority developed an art music exclusively for their own class. It acted as entertainment, and also as a patronized and carefully controlled vehicle for the aspirations of that same class, given form by composers who ranged from the status of creative genius to dullard. It speaks well of us all that the music of the creative genius seems to survive, though often having to stand a long test of time before it is appreciated. Thus the individual genius in art music flies frequently far ahead of the consciousness of its patron class, and indeed of the general mass of people.

Underpinning this tiny stratum of art music, in which we may include for general purposes Western religious music (though this is not a strict inclusion as religious music has a number of elusive sources both historically and creatively), was a far greater body of music. This was, and is, the music and song perpetuated in daily life by the majority of the population. In past centuries this was almost entirely the collective ethnic or folk music of any region or culture.

With the increasing development of cities, ordinary people created a city-based entertainment music of their own. This urban music was not part of the collective ethnic music found throughout the region or the land, but was in many ways still stylistically based upon it. The foundations of national or regional music are sacred or magical; they are expressions of the human relationship to the land, to life, to death, to the seasons. The elemental vocalization or instrumental patterns of regional and national music emerge from the deepest levels of consciousness, to be shaped through human interaction with the land itself. This is why ethnic musics worldwide share many rhythms and patterns of melody in common, yet are quite distinct from one another.

With the increase of industrialization, the industrial working classes developed an entertainment music, and in many areas a specific religious music, entirely their own, relatively isolated from the ethnic music of their region but not in any way antagonistic to it. Many new waves of popular music developed, based upon dances, upon musical styles gradually developing in other countries and eventually being imported, and upon the advent of new musical instruments. In many households the ethnic or folk music existed comfortably side by side with popular entertainment; this co-existence was maintained in European/American culture well into the era of radio.

Mass media, however, gave a tremendous increase to the speed at which popular entertainment changed, and the rate at which it could be communicated to large numbers of people. By this time, in the middle of the twentieth century, original folk or regional musics were already dying out in Western culture, though they had been in decline for a century or more.

But the advent of the record player and of television, the opportunity to have visual and auditory entertainment cheaply in any home, suddenly meant that manipulation of the mass musical consciousness as a market, rather than as an organic development that took its own course, was eminently possible.

Within a very short period of time, no more than two generations, technology has radically adjusted the collective concepts of music, the shared musical experience. It is easy, of course, to say that this is a negative series of events ... just as it is easy to say that this ferment of trivia ushers in a New Age. Perhaps we will know the truth when the Age of Aquarius really does begin, more than a century from now.

## Elements and Product

I have repeatedly asserted throughout this book that there is an inherent Elemental power which all and any of us may express as music. Furthermore, by the natural events of universal proportions, there is within music in general an Elemental correspondence or resonance, which may be used to good or ill effect. Whenever we listen to music, any music of any sort, we are directly experiencing Elemental patterns and frequencies. This matter of direct experience is important: music stimulates and resonates with the Elements within our body-psychic complex, our whole entity. This is not simply a theory of certain music making us feel airy, watery, or earthy, or of stimulating typical planetary or landscape images, or of primal nature forces; these are all extras.

The foundation of music is, in itself, by the very nature of reiterated patterns, proportions, and selected overtones and frequencies, an utterance of the Four Elements. Some such patterns and frequencies are more potent than others, for they attune to relatively pure Elemental energies, or to frequencies inherent within our own entities, our body and psyche, to other life forms, and to certain geomantic forces.

The model of the Four Elements is not merely a convenient tradition of explication but is found at the very roots of our awareness. It is, in mystical or metaphysical terms, the foundation, the universe.

During each successive century or phase of human development, music has appeared in various formalized expressions: the music of the state, of religion, of entertainment, and of wealth and patronage. This last category in particular became what we now loosely term 'art' music, though art music also applies to political and religious music in most cases. Meanwhile, ordinary people continued to make music, often drawing upon extensive and surprisingly profound oral musical traditions that have little in common with art music. This music is based upon Elemental energies shaped by tradition rather than by individual creative skill. Such a tradition is defined by the interaction between the people and their land or region; this premise applies worldwide.

Clearly such a simplified picture cannot be applicable today, particularly in the West. We do indeed find well-defined ethnic music in certain sectors of the population, often far removed from any native or original land, as in the case of black roots music or Asian or Oriental music, all of which are well established and thriving throughout Europe and America.

There is little left in the way of European ethnic music, for we cannot, even with the most sympathetic attitude, call folk-music revivalism truly ethnic or collective. Such ethnic musics do indeed survive, often aided by the state, in Eastern European countries, and in some isolated regions of Western Europe, but they are a tiny and dying minority.

In America the situation is slightly different, as the native music was that of the American Indians, and was mostly but not entirely destroyed by invading militaristic interests and settlers from Europe. When various European ethnic groups entered America (North or South), their own music came with them, and was gradually modified by interaction with the land through several centuries.

We can see this modification at work, for example, in the melodic shape of folk ballads and instrumental music that exists in both native European and American versions. Certain folk-music collectors during the early years of the twentieth century were able to examine such music on both sides of the Atlantic. The subject of comparison is vast, and can be highly technical, but there are very distinct American variants of instrumental music preserved also in Europe (such as Scottish or Irish dance music) and of songs and ballads, particularly of the ancient ballads that once underpinned European culture as vehicles of poetry, melody, and mythic imagery. In short, we hear the same song or melody, often with the same name and general content, but the style is quite distinctly American or European, and instantly recognizable.

It is occasionally argued that such modifications represent either the influence of black music in America upon white folk music, or that American variants represent older forms that remained relatively unmodified. Neither of these arguments stands up well, though there may be elements of truth in both. The characteristic of ethnic musics or true folk music is always resonant of the land first, then of the culture and way of life of the people, and finally of racial interaction and influence. This is why we would never confuse the music of, say, Spain and Japan with one another, or even American reels with Irish reels, to quote two much closer relatives. The land speaks through the music, which is modified by the lives and social customs of humans within that land.

It might be true to say today that the remaining folk music of the Western world is that vast sector of popular entertainment generally called 'country' music. It combines white, black, and ethnic musics into a popular and simple vehicle that expresses basic emotions. As a result of this homogeneous quality, it is popular all over the planet, but especially in America and Europe. The influence of country music can be heard in the popular musics of Africa, Japan, and China, and many other unlikely places, often mingling with true ethnic styles and forms. Its very homogeneous nature, however, also makes it repetitive and unacceptable to many people, and it is mainly a product music today, at least in America and Europe, just as any other popular music is a product.

We have been repeatedly told in the press and in many books on music that first jazz, then rock (especially rock) was the new music of the people, enthroned by popular approval and demand. If we rely on statistics and general popularity and accessibility, then it has to be admitted that country music beats rock music in both long- and short-term levels of popularity and demand. There is no space in a book of this sort to start dissecting interactions and fusions between rock, country music, and jazz, many of which have been very fruitful indeed. Such fusions work, however, only when they are deeply motivated and genuinely creative; if they are merely an intellectual exercise or experiment, they always fail.

The reader will be relieved to know, at this stage, that I do not propose an esoteric theory of Country Music; I would merely say that this general commercial music, with very simple styles and limitations, has replaced, entirely through the communication of mass media, the more complex and subtle ethnic musics of the West. Whether we like it or not, country music, rock, and popular music in general are the closest that the Western world has to an Elemental music in general circulation.

Obviously when we delve deeper we find ethnic musics, and when we delve even deeper we find spiritual and magical musical traditions. But there is no general vehicle for empowerment through music, vast as our musical immediacy and product are. The general satisfaction felt by millions of people listening to very simple music forms, such as are found in country or rock or pop (when analysed divorced from their overt social or commercialized, emotional appeal), is due to the reiteration of Elemental patterns. Nothing more, nothing less.

In this book some very specific techniques are offered for practical work employing Elemental patterns of music: these are placed in the broader context of visualization, meditation, mediation of inner power, and the perennial traditions concerning universal music and its effect upon and through humanity. In popular music the Elemental patterns are usually random, though some, such as those of rock music, have become highly stereotyped. They are recognized to a limited extent consciously, as the formulae which artists, songwriters, arrangers, and record producers apply to generate reactions among an often undiscriminating buying public.

But in the remnants of spiritual and magical music worldwide, the Elemental patterns are intentionally affirmed and dedicated within a chosen tradition. They are aligned to images, such as gods and goddesses, and in some primal traditions form part of long epic tales that have a mythic and sacred power, dealing with the creation of the universe and its inhabitants.

More specifically, Elemental music can operate upon the power centres or *chakras*, the much-discussed, little-understood nodes of energy within the human body. In musical empowerment, we should seek musical patterns that act upon these centres, and bring them into harmony with their universal octaves. This means exposing one's inner self to the holism of land, planet, solar system, and eventually the stellar universe. It all sounds extremely grandiose when stated as mere words, but through the octave and harmonic properties of our universe, which extend right into the genetics of the human body, it is a profound possibility.

# 2 Ancient Temple Music

What might we expect to have heard, to have undertaken for ourselves, in an ancient temple using the power of sound? How would this compare with the individual arts such as those of the solitary seer, mystic, shaman, or magician? The sole training remaining today in the Western world, with the possible exception of Gregorian plainchant, is that of the hidden or underground traditions. There is no fully comparable tuition to that of the ancient temples and their vast traditions; we have only fragments.

In the East, however, such traditions survived formally in a more coherent state well into the twentieth century, and though there are many significant differences (often passed over or ignored by Western writers), we may draw certain informative parallels. The most important part of such traditions, however, is always the oral personal tuition and experience. Deeply conservative tradition will frequently preserve detailed forms with little or no elucidation upon their content. So we always need a combination of exoteric vehicle, which is the formalized teaching and spiritual tradition, and esoteric empowerment, the initiatory and specific instructions, the keys that permit the vehicle to come alive.

Without this benefit of experience and clarification, which comes directly from an individual or group working seriously within a system and tradition, all other study and research is valueless. No amount of library research, intellectual, historical, and textual analysis, no amount of music theory or comparative musicology, can empower the inner heart of music.

Such empowerment comes from dedicated and disciplined working in meditation, visualization, utterance of tones and chants, and in certain conditions from sacred dance. But before we can use these techniques, and reassess and develop them for the twenty-first century, we need to be able to listen, to hear the inner music that is uttered within us perpetually. This book attempts to pass on to the reader some of the teachings and methods of the esoteric traditions concerning music, and to make some helpful comparisons between these and a number of significant modern developments which reaffirm ancient tradition in the light of materialist science.

Rather than delve into a long series of textual and academic music-ological comparisons, let us approach our question, 'What might we have heard and undertaken in an ancient temple concerning music, power, and harmony?', in an imaginative way. By imaginative, however, we must not assume anything frivolous or fantastical: the arts and disciplines which will be outlined are all firmly grounded in experience, tradition, and practical work. They may be compared favourably with a large number of historical accounts, texts, techniques, and treatises, from both the West and the East. So many books exist today that recount such sources or reassess them without going into practical experiential detail that there is simply no need to repeat this kind of valuable source work here. Let us, therefore, go straight to the temple, and begin.

## Keeping the World in Tune

The purpose of the ancient schools and temples, whose traditions survive in various magical orders and in ethnic or folk practices even today (though in an attenuated form), was to *keep the world in tune,* and to keep humanity in tune with the world. The world means not only our immediate physical planet but also the greater world of the solar system, and then of the universe.

This may seem a simplistic, even grandiose, suggestion, so let us consider the planetary background to such a fundamental and important statement. We must first imagine, or perhaps remember, that the world was not permeated by electronic resonances, fields, or vibrations as it is today. There was no barrage of noise either in an acoustic format from speakers or in a transmitted format as radiating signals. The foundation of the metaphysical and magical arts of the ancient temples and schools was not one of generating transmissions (whether mental or technological) but of attuning to the existing planetary and cosmic resonances and patterns.

These patterns, musical sounds existing within and beyond the normal range of hearing, were harmonics of solar, lunar, planetary, and stellar utterances. Each entity, each planet, generates or utters a sound, a statement, a pattern of energy. These resonate within one another, and generate waves through the universe. In planetary terms, the utterance voice or tone of the planet is modified by the orbital passage through the field of the sun and other planets of the solar system. They are all modified, in one way or another, by interaction with other stars. In this context we need to remember that the Earth and Moon, in esoteric tradition, are one *world,* the Lunar World; this is consubstantial with, or harmonized within, the great Solar World, of Sun and Planets (the solar system). This in turn is within the Stellar World, the universe. Thus all Three Worlds are, in truth, One World, one universe.

The physical planets of our solar system, like the sun and stars, are *nodes* or locations generated from the interaction of many fields of energy in multifold dimensions. Wherever such fields or resonates intersect, they create a localized pattern or node through the interaction of their various tones and harmonics: these are the stars that appear in space, and the planets that rotate in holistic or harmonic patterns around the stars. This is, of course, the inverse of materialist physics, in which the stars themselves utter the energies, rather than appear as nodes uttered by the energies. Both models are admissible within esoteric metaphysics, for the appearance of nodes (stars or planets) modifies the resonance of the interacting energies, creating the utterances of the stars which we study in modern physics. The metaphysical utterances have long been studied in deep contemplation, through astrology and through inner listening.

In environmental terms, a location, a land, or an entire continent produces a sound of its own. The broad remnant of this today is, of course, the national or ethnic music of specific peoples. In this type of music, the interaction is between humanity and the land in which they have lived for many generations. This is, in fact, a very important example of the concept of interaction in music, environment, energy, and consciousness, and is frequently passed over by theorists who seek to find higher abstract forms without ever considering real or fundamental patterns.

## Re-creating the World

In certain Eastern religious rituals, even today, we find a venerable tradition of *re-creating the world*: this also appears in magical arts, folk customs, and primal ceremonies worldwide. The basis of this practice is simple but profound: to pause, to cease, and then renew. In the ancient temples, sound, uttered in harmonic patterns as music, was the primary vehicle for this art of renovation. To understand the principles behind this, and to apply them within ourselves, we need to pursue a teaching of sound, resonance, and pattern.

The musical utterances of the universe begin with the primal voice, the Sound of Being. This sound resonates and proliferates in an increasingly

Figure 1

# The Four Elements

The Four Elements of Air, Fire, Water, and Earth, act as a conceptual model at the foundation of a holistic or unified perception. When music is related to the Four Elements, we should consider *relative states of energy*. The Elements are always related in sets or rotations of four relative states: each Element has within itself a fourfold cycle of Four Elements, and the relative image can never be reduced to ultimate units or isolated 'pure' Elements.

This mirroring process is found in the nature of music, which never consists of 'pure' notes, but of relative patterns, each note being composed of large numbers of relative harmonics or overtones. A full cycle of Elements gives the musical proportions that manifest as the Octave. (See also Figure 2.)

EARTH is the most substantial or solid in any set or rotation of Four Elements: WATER is relatively less solid and more fluid: FIRE is active and incandescent: AIR is the least substantial and most active. The Four Elements should not be confused with physical air, fire, water and earth, which act as examples of relative conditions.

Musically a simple Elemental model is found through the steps or scales of pitch: Earth is the lowest in pitch, Water one step above Earth, Fire one step above Water, Air one step above Fire. In the standard musical scale this relative pattern of pitch gives rise to a well-defined number of proportions that have a natural or universal validity, occurring in many relative states or conditions. A list of relative attributes for the Four Elements would be as follows:


*Air:* Beginning/Birth/Inception/First Breath/Dawn/Morning/
Childhood/Sunrise/Thinking/Questioning/Emerging/Arising/*Sword*/
Arrow/Cutting/Flying/Moving/Liberty/Leaping/Exciting/*Life*/Wind/
Fresh/Power/Sound/Spring/Germination/Inspiration/Attention.
*Vowel sound: E.*

*Fire:* Increasing/Adulthood/Continuing/Exhalation/Noon/Brightness/
Ability/Zenith/Directing/Controlling/Incandescent/Burning/*Rod*/
Ruling/Balancing/Upright/Seeing/Relating/Harmonizing/*Light*/Flame/
Heat/Energy/Colour/Summer/Growth/Illumination/Perception.
*Vowel sound: I.*

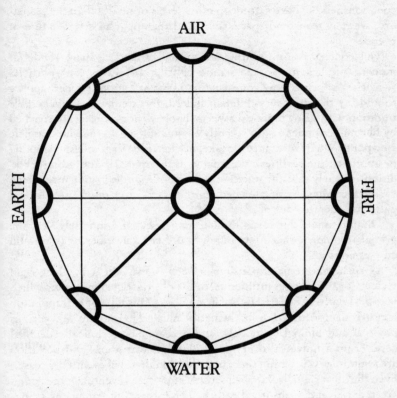

*Water:* Fulfilling/Maturity/Culminating/Second Breath/Evening/
Ending/Fullness/Sunset/Feeling/Receiving/Settling/Flowing/*Cup*/
Giving/Purifying/Sustaining/Nourishing/Cleansing/Clarifying/
Emotion/*Love*/Autumn/Harvest/Sharing/Intuition.
*Vowel sound: O.*

*Earth:* Ceasing/Age/Rest/Exhalation/Night/Darkness/Peace/Starlight/
Supporting/Reflecting/Solidify/Manifesting/*Shield*/Mirror/Returning/
Grace/Coldness/Dryness/Containment/Touch/*Law*/Winter/Waiting/
Preserving/Expression.
*Vowel sound: A.*

expanding spiral or spherical field of interaction, generating space, time, and events. *The difference between space, time, and events is a property of human consciousness upon a planet, and not a reality in itself.* If our consciousness is able to attune to other levels or modes than the planetary, we may transcend space, time, and the apparent serial nature of events.

This concept is not too different to that of the 'Big Bang' model of modern physics, or to the subtle concept of waves and particles (wavicles) which is now commanding much attention. Or perhaps we should say that it is very different indeed, for it embodies a venerable tradition with many practical aspects that have not yet been approached by our modern sciences, so recently emerging from a crude mechanistic viewpoint. Whatever stance we take, modern physics is at last beginning to approach the realities long taught in the spiritual and esoteric traditions: namely that the universe consists of a unified resonance which varies according to open-ended, unrestricted, and multi-dimensional patterns generated out of itself.

The utterance, the voice, the harmonics, expand infinitely. Yet the primal resonance, that first Sound, is present and inherent in all and any ramifications.

As such, harmonic expansion is open-ended, not a fixed or rigid system; it can and does proliferate, or may be restricted in subsets which become relatively isolated or unharmonious. This type of extrapolation is clearly demonstrated by mathematics, musical harmonics, and various physical and biological models, and need not be technically detailed here. From a universal overview, isolation, corruption, and pollution are temporary (i.e. within time, of a duration that will eventually cease). Even the most rigid, isolated structures or patterns eventually break and are reduced and reabsorbed into higher forms. But for us, as beings living partially within time, upon a planet resonating to the energy of a star and orbiting around that star in harmony with other planets, such a cosmic overview is too often used as an idle consolation, a sop, rather than as a true vision transcending time. We need also to be able to cope with imbalance, disharmony, and follow that inner harmony which tells us how to readjust.

Humanity has the ability to initiate patterns which harmonize, or conflict, with the expanding, open-ended resonance of the universe. In the ancient temples, the primary purpose of training was to keep the cycles, the patterns, harmonious without rigidity. In modern technology we seem to have imprisoned ourselves in antagonistic patterns, resonances devised to exclude those of the environment, the planet, the solar system, the universe. We have, in short, exteriorized and extrapolated certain resonances, certain patterns, towards their ultimate redundancy. And finally we discover that we are making ourselves redundant, generating our own dawnless night, springless winter, and collective destruction, by shutting out the rejuvenating, vitalizing Sound which energizes, empowers, and permits us to be free.

Ancient temple arts and disciplines were complex, but the main training was concerned with uttering and perfecting tones, empowered sounds, which reattuned specific natural resonances that were potentially or actually drifting out of harmony with the broader cycles and patterns of Planet, Solar System, Universe.

Similar empowered sounds were uttered to open the way, usher in, or aid in the birth and development of energies, patterns, and life forms. The traditional model is one of a series of archetypes or matrices, shapes which appear in a harmonic series. This series enables forces to resonate through universal, stellar, planetary, and organic and inorganic forms. We might visualize such shapes as fitting within one another, following patterns of relative proportion defined, for us, by musical facts such as the law of octaves. This law simply reveals, even to the most unmusical person, that a note one octave above or below another is clearly the same note in a relatively higher or lower form. The law of octaves is one of the fundamental universal laws, expressed audibly for us in musical sound, present in all wave or particle patterns, present in all aspects of time, space, energy, and events. A cosmology of this sort is found in a famous passage by Plato, which is quoted and examined in Appendix 3.

To localize the practical aspects of empowered sound, we might take a typical small example, such as a geomantic problem. A location such as a spring or area of forest becomes unhealthy, polluted, de-energized. In modern practice we might purify through chemicals, through irradiation, through severe pruning, digging, pumping, filtering, and so forth. Many of these methods are highly effective, particularly as short-term emergency measures.

But the esoteric traditions, equally practical, would first consider how this location became detuned, why it had developed an unharmonious, unhealthy resonance. If we liken our theoretical location to a spinning zone or field of energy (a quite acceptable model in modern technological terms), it has been knocked out of balance. A specific resonance, sound, or, in the case of temple training, a chant or musical utterance will set it back into harmony again. If this fails, the more potent practice of unsinging, pausing, and re-creating might be undertaken.

Our imaginative example, eminently practical, serves only as a local model. In fact temple training consisted mainly of finding and uttering tones which harmonized the land in such a way that illness or imbalances did not occur in the first place.

Temple music consisted of cycles and utterances in rhythmic patterns: the rhythms were not simply those of the music itself, though these were studied and developed in depth, but rhythms over a longer temporal period. Thus an overview of spiritual music would include utterances of brief duration, but these would be part of, harmonized within, the greater music of months, years, planetary cycles, even of stellar duration.

A typical annual cycle would consist of music for the Seasons: empowered tones and patterns uttered at the turning-points, the opening of the gates between Winter, Spring, Summer, and Autumn. These initial utterances would be modified according to stellar patterns: certain constellations rise and move through the regional sky or planetary sphere of observation in regular patterns; others appear and disappear over longer timescales.

Within this annual and perennial cycle, subcycles would be intoned. These related to the regular orbits and appearances over the horizon of specific planets, the Moon, and the subtle earth-tides or geomagnetic fluxes. Within the monthly cycles, daily utterance were made, attuning to the passage of the Sun, the Moon, the Planets, and the cycle of atmosphere, weather, the passage of animals across the land, and the growth of crops; all of these were also incorporated, enharmonized, in the broader cycles listed above.

Before exploring practical methods for the present day, we should examine this holistic overview, which provides an important framework of support and balance for our developing awareness.

# 3  Harmonics and Hierarchies

Many of the traditional systems of esoteric training and philosophy employ a hierarchical model. This method – indeed, this philosophical or metaphysical view of the universe – is frequently abused and mis-understood. Approaching the twenty-first century as we are, many of the concepts of hierarchy in spiritual disciplines or arts are clearly unacceptable, mainly due to their blatant corruption within political religion, and its negative repressive ramifications within modern society. But this unacceptability also runs through esoteric groups or orders, and is found in many self-styled New Age modern structures: the concept of a hierarchy is frequently employed for the gaining and retention of individual power. Thus the true meaning and purpose of hierarchy in a universal sense becomes corrupted into that of temporal authority.

At one time the corruption was hidden within the hierarchy of church and state; such corruption is now open and known. Today we should be more concerned over the hierarchy of the guru, the spiritual teacher, the psychoanalyst, and of the channeller who claims to be able to mediate intelligence from entities in other dimensions. All such hier-archies depend upon a linear attitude, one in which there are 'superior' and 'inferior' levels with connecting (or separating) lines of com-munication or energy.

Let us consider the traditional teaching concerning hierarchies, and then compare hierarchies and harmonics. While hierarchy is an uncomfortable and corruptible concept, harmonics open our awareness to resonances and relationships between patterns, between apparently disparate entities, giving them an order without connotation of spurious authority.

As has been said repeatedly, a musical model of reality, in which we hear and resonate in harmony with our environment (which ultimately is universal), is a creative and unifying model. This unity or harmony was once inherent in concepts of hierarchy in ancient cultures, but it acquired a series of false values and implications with the development

Figure 2

# The Spiral of Octaves

The Four Elements relate in many ways, giving rise to fundamental patterns and proportions that are readily found in nature, ranging from generally observed phases and concepts to the detailed laws of modern physics. An initial approach to this holism or interpenetrating set of relationships is to use rotation, the model of an expanding spiral. This occurs in music as the expanding spiral of Fifths and Octaves. Such rotation is found in many levels or ranges of universal proportion, from genetic material and sub-atomic patterns, to the orbiting of planets around a star, to the rotation of galaxies. The relative states are traditionally defined in sets of concepts, as in our Figure 1. Our illustration is necessarily a flat one, due to the limits of the printed page, but the expanding spiral is really multi-dimensional. The two-dimensional spiral, and similar 'flat' models used in training of consciousness for meditation and conceptual development are always simple variants of three dimensional models, relating to the Six Directions (Figure 7). The simple variants enable us to grasp certain patterns of relationship, but are never regarded as dogmatic or pseudo-scientific 'proofs', merely as working models or interim symbols acting as aids to understanding.

Commencing with a chosen lowest note for Earth, defined here as C1, the rotation of the Elements gradually expands in an opening spiral, and ascends in pitch. During each step many relative harmonic proportions arise. The initial steps, 1234 or CDEF in a standard major scale, represent one rotation of Elements. In these four steps, the upper half of the scale, 5678 or GABC is inherent and unavoidably uttered as a set of overtones. This mirroring, or overtone phenomena, runs through all music.

The relative state of the Elements is demonstrated by the music spiral: one octave above our initial Earth or C1 is a new scale commencing with the Element of Air or C8. The note C does not reoccur as Earth again until C29. This Octave of octaves, shown in our figure, corresponds to the general range of human hearing, which is in itself a mirror or harmonic of the universal law of octaves.

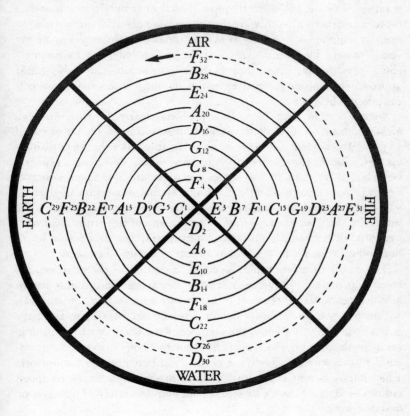

of rational or materialistic scientific thought. The problem of hierarchies is deeply embedded in esoteric literature, for example, and is partly demonstrated by the teaching models that developed with the advent of printing. Illustrations were frequently used in temple training and in esoteric instruction worldwide, but these were always, without exception, accompanied by personal instruction. Once the oral instruction was removed, by the circulation of the printed page, an increasingly spurious scientism crept into esoteric instruction; this false linear approach has often reached extremes in nineteenth- and twentieth-century publications.

Some examples demonstrate the problem clearly. In many magical, alchemical, or mystical texts, we find illustrations which are intended to guide the student. These, almost invariably, take the form of hierarchies. The linear nature of sight, presenting object and separate observer, is inherent in two-dimensional illustrations. Such concepts depend upon separation, space. Thus a spatial dimension is given to spiritual concepts that are not inherently or exclusively spatial. The hierarchy then becomes a series of separated entities with linear connections, rather than a mutually interpenetrating, inseparable set of harmonics, which is how it would appear in a musical example.

The ratios or relationships selected in nature, in the universe, are those which we find inherently musical; we recognize certain patterns as music because they resonate or harmonize with certain fundamentals within our own consciousness, our bioelectrical entity, the land, the living creatures, the planet, the stars. Modern sciences such as holography or the new physics repeatedly show this holistic harmonic prevalence in the universe. They are *musical entities,* because the universe which they examine is musical. The old materialist sciences are linear entities, acting as models of separation, and ultimately of antagonism and destruction.

It seems likely that the 'rational' sciences of the eighteenth and nineteenth centuries will soon be looked upon as temporary aberrations, aberrations for which we may yet pay the extreme price of self-destruction. It was suggested to me, during a conversation with a teacher of American-Indian traditions, that this time will perhaps be known as 'The Very Dark Ages'.

The holistic nature of music is greatly disguised at present by the contemporary nature of the music score, a set of dots moving in a linear manner across a spatial grid, the stave upon the page. This visual-presentation music may be useful for certain types of performance, but it defeats our inner sense of wholeness, and eventually cheats the customary sight-reader of much of his or her innate memory and hearing of music.

In *The Third Ear*,[3] a remarkable book by Joachim-Ernst Berendt, many of these inherently cultural problems relating to music and listening are discussed in depth. Berendt cites, for example, a study made of Western musicians and composers in which it seems, from the evidence collected, that their musicality had been reconditioned to the left-hand side of the brain. In nature musicality and other creative functions and abilities are properties of the right brain.

The subject of harmonics and hierarchies runs through much of the material in our following chapters, and the reader should always bear in mind that a hierarchy is not a system of superiority or inferiority, but of harmonic or proportional relationships.

# 4   Images and Inspiration

Composers and musicians worldwide draw their inspiration from a great variety of sources; some of the dynamics and polarities of this process are outlined in Chapters 9–10, which summarize traditional esoteric teachings on the subject. Musical inspiration, education, and initiation, however, were at one time connected to specific gods and goddesses, and very precise magical and spiritual techniques may be defined in this context.

At the simplest level we know that an image or *telesma* of a divinity or innerworld contact connected to music can be highly beneficial and energizing in meditation and visualization. Thus such images may be employed as inspirational guides for the composer; such a technique does not, at least on the surface, pose any problems of acceptability to the modern mind, though its older variants may seem unnecessarily complex and time-consuming.

The deeper levels and techniques of using imagery to gain spiritual insight or inspiration, however, are firmly rooted in esoteric arts and disciplines. A more ancient manifestation of the art of telesmatic images or god-forms and music, more likely to be confusing or even disturbing to the modern individual, is that of a powerful god or goddess over-looking or overshadowing a musician or group of musicians. Both of the terms used are slightly unfortunate, though they are common in modern publications that deal with such subjects as magical arts, mediation (as opposed to meditation) and, more fashionably at present, 'channelling'. It would be healthier, and more precise, to suggest that this psychic phenomenon consists of the meditator musician or group temporarily resonating within the imaginative form, god or goddess image, or telesmatic image. This is, of course, a musical concept.

We shall return to this concept and its practice later, for it is one of the major traditional arts of musical empowerment, and provided it is correctly understood and undertaken, offers enormous potential. It is maintained today mainly in folk practices in the West, in a very attenuated form, but persists quite actively within the collective classical and religious musics of the East and in Africa.

Before extending our exploration into restatements of the more powerful ancient techniques for modern use, we need to consider the basic method, in which an image of some sort provides a focus of inspiration and energy for music. There are many complex refinements of such a basic method, some of which follow shortly.

In religious music, even that of orthodox Christianity, application to carefully defined images plays a major role, and this is perhaps that religion's closest connection both to the musical and magical techniques of the ancient pagan world and to the living practices of other world religions. In art music, however, the formal concept of inspiration by image is seldom encountered, but images arise nevertheless. We are not talking here about composers choosing a symbol or an image and writing around it, but about the far deeper, more empowering event in which an image spontaneously appears, even forces itself, and may not be denied within the imagination. Many composers recount incidents of this sort; dreams in which a person appears and plays music, feelings of powerful communication from mythic sources while writing, and so forth.

A standard 'explanation' of this phenomenon in terms of modern psychology is likely to include reference to the subconscious or unconscious mind, and perhaps to archetypes in the incorrect Jungian redefinition of the word. C. G. Jung's ambiguity in defining archetypes is discussed in Dane Rudyhar's book *The Magic of Tone and the Art of Music*.[4] At the opposite extreme we have the very fashionable subject of channelling, in which inspiration is supposedly derived from beings in other dimensions, with little or no allowance for human perception, intelligence, or discretion. Channelling is, of course, no more nor less than good old-fashioned mediumship, as defined by Madame H. P. Blavatsky in the nineteenth century when she initiated the spiritualist movement, before moving on to greater things with the highly influential but now virtually defunct Theosophical Society.

There seem to be very attractive connections between a Jungian interpretation of the psyche, the modern practice of mediumship or channelling, and the known arts and disciplines of mysticism, spiritual development, and specific practices of the ancient temples and enduring magical orders. Such seeming connections, however, are superficial, for the magical and perennial spiritual traditions employ images, archetypes, and innerworld or spirit contacts in a manner that is clearly defined, and different in many ways from either the psychological materialist, or spiritualist models of inspiration and psychic communication. This is not to suggest that all 'spirit' communication in the ancient world or in earlier centuries was of a higher order than at present: that would be nonsense, and there can be no doubt that trivial and debased practices exist in every century. What it really implies is that modern spiritism or channelling lacks the philosophy, wisdom, and practical techniques that were so highly developed in the ancient temples, and which are, to greater or lesser degrees, preserved in the esoteric traditions, requiring long years of training and discipline.

In Chapter 5 a guided visualization is included which offers one modern way of using the perennial imaginative techniques in the context of both a god-form, Apollo, and musical transformation. It would be quite reasonable to go straight to this exercise, and work with it immediately upon a practical, experiential level, either by reading aloud or by using the accompanying cassette recording.[20] But for those who are concerned with the foundations and background to the technique, some further discussion might be helpful before proceeding to practical work. Let us examine some aspects of both practice and theory concerning images which may be used for musical inspiration, enlightenment, and empowerment.

## Inspiration and Interaction

Our positive musical response to images is usually thought of as inspiration: the image is supposed to inspire us to make music of some sort (a landscape, a theme, a lover, a myth, a divinity). Conversely, inspired and skilful music can generate images within our awareness, stimulating the imagination with its power.

But there is also an interaction between image and creation of music, and music and creation of images (be it as a composer, listener, or performer), which must be given attention. This art was well known in the ancient world, and is still used in a very defined manner in advanced magical arts today. It works in the following manner.

If we give attention to an image, we build it within our imagination. The form is more or less similar to its general presentation in the collective imagination, which simply means that everyone sees the image in approximately the same way and that its entirety is shared collectively and anonymously, often with roots extending far back in apparent serial time. Such an image need not be (and seldom is) exactly identical in every individual imagination. By entertaining the image, which is to say receiving it into our field of imagination, we not only draw it into ourselves but also give of our inherent energy to it: the imaginative process is mutual, relative, and interactive. This is one of the great 'secrets' of successful magic.

The dynamics of this process have long been known, and are frequently abused by religious and political rabble-rousers, employing oratory combined with music to whip crowds into a frenzy of imbalance and destruction. When the negative aspects of this process are supported by a state religion, they can be effective for centuries. Music, oratory, and rhythm play an important part in the feedback process.

There is a definable growth or transformation of the key images, rhythms, and patterns that affect the collective imagination, thereby working upon individuals and groups. If we consider, for example, the patriotic, militaristic, nationalistic music of only one or two generations previous (say, from the late nineteenth century to the 1950s), it seems crude, weak, and ineffectual, an almost blatant, crass medium for mass manipulation. Yet it had enormous power and effect, driving people into war and death, upholding spurious religious and political values aimed solely at the preservation of a ruling élite. Whatever effect it had upon the people of its day, Victorian patriotic music, and derivative militaristic music through to the middle of the twentieth century, has little of its original effect today upon Western culture.

We also have, however, a very refined science of combining images and music in the pop-music video and television commercial. These short, powerful entities of combined music and imagery are painstakingly constructed for maximum effect.

Whereas the patriotic, propagandist music of our grandparents was designed to filter out to as many people as possible and have a lasting, binding effect upon the imagination, creating a group or collective will (or perhaps we might say lack of true will), the aims of the pop-music video are more ephemeral and diffuse, though no less powerful and corrupt. They aim to steer the consumer towards certain trends, certain purchases, for a strictly limited period of time, then become invalid and unattractive as the next temporary conditioning pattern, allied with images and music, is set in motion.

The apparent unification of communication which arises from mass media and instant accessibility to entertainment and information actually leads to increasing isolation and fragmentation. This fragmentation of the collective and individual imagination is greatly accelerated by our reliance upon technology to replace our inner faculties.

The comparison between the propagandist music and imagery of the last century and the prostituting, suggestive music and imagery of the television commercial or pop video reveals by crude example how rapidly our imagination and its response to music has altered in only 100 years. We should also ask, and perhaps meditate upon, whether or not the videos of today would have had their designed effect upon our grandparents or great-grandparents. Just as their musical propaganda and imagery seem crude to us, perhaps our so-sophisticated triggers and manipulating musics might seem incomprehensible, or merely gross, to them. This is not an idle or flippant question, and meditation upon such comparisons gives extensive insight into the power of music, imagery, and its transformation through human culture.

There is a meditative exercise connected to this concept, in which we attune to the music of one cultural period and then attempt to visualize how it might have worked in an earlier era. This is the reverse of our standard imaginative exercise, where we try to bring the music of past eras to life for the present day and it has some surprising results.

Let us draw our attention away from the crudest or potentially negative levels of the phenomenon of imagery and interchange, such as militaristic or pop-video music, and consider the subject in a more precise manner. If an image is carefully selected and defined, it acts as an interactive interface for energy.

The most potent images are those which are drawn from true archetypes; in other words, they represent something of the universe through their form as presented to us. When we visualize such images, we draw them into our sphere of energy; we draw power from them and we give of our vital energies to them.

In idealized circumstances, an image of this sort will exchange considerable amounts of energy, taking in human imaginative forces, and modifying and returning the archetypical or universal forces that it embodies. This process works very effectively with music, and a major key to the power of music to arouse energies, images, and reactions within us rests within this concept of archetypical interchange.

We may distinguish between several different levels or types of inner communication involving music:

1. Gods and goddesses of music and related subjects such as poetry, dance, therapy, and mathematics or cosmology. Though these subjects have long been separated in modern study, they were originally inseparable. Curiously, many of our new scientific developments are beginning to reassess the mythic and practical fusion of scientific arts.

2. Specific teaching or inspirational contacts. These include dream persons who teach music or musical skills, innerworld beings or

masters who give tuition during visualization and meditation, and specific contacts or guides who actually overshadow or attune to musicians during performance

All of this second broad category may be undertaken through application to specific god or goddess images, as in 1), but frequently occurs as contact with other entities or intelligences. These may be inherent within a spiritual or magical tradition, such as male or female saints, innerworld adepts or priests and priestesses, and specific teaching masters within ethnic musical traditions. St Cecilia, for example, is a Christian saint concerned especially with music; the bardic order in ancient Celtic Europe was concerned with poetry and music; Homer was not only a historical person but the perfected mythic epic poet and singer, and so forth.

This last category was of considerable importance worldwide, and still occurs in many traditions. In the West we have the powerful tradition of learning music and musical skills from the Fairies: these are a people with many subtle arts, living in a dimension or underworld close to our own. They are often conflated with the concept of ancestors or revered teachers who are innerworld parents to the tribe, clan, or land. In ancient tradition, some kings and queens have the role of inventors or teachers of the arts, including music.

A much later corruption of this primal tradition is that in which blues guitarists or folk fiddle players learned their skills from the Devil, whom they meet at a crossroads at midnight. This is nothing more than a superstitious replacement of the older tradition of learning from innerworld sources with scaremongering propaganda – though no doubt skilled musicians in isolated communities may have enjoyed their notoriety, just as they do today in city-based cultures. The inspiration, however, remains real.

Much of the Christian propaganda concerning music revolves around the Fairies and the Devil: this is an echo of pagan traditions of learning music from otherworldly beings, connected to geomantic sites such as springs, wells, hills, forests, ancient sacred sites such as stone circles, mounds, and standing stones. In Britain and Europe, many stone circles or collections of megalithic stones have a legend attached them to the effect that they are dancers turned to stone by dancing on a Sunday or saint's day. How did they merit such punishment? Because their musician was none other than the Devil in disguise, who filled them with such dancing frenzy that they danced all through Saturday night, unknowing, into the Sunday morning.

This may seem like propagandist nonsense, but it reflects a number of important traditions concerning music and sacred sites, not least of which is the one that they were used by ordinary people for music and dancing ceremonies well into the Christian era. I am not, incidentally, referring here to 'witchcraft', for that is another complex discussion in its own right, but simply to folk and regional practices of carrying out dance ceremonies at prehistoric sites. A few of these dances with attendant rituals still persist in British and European folklore to this day.

The Devil, the *deo falsus*, is simply a corrupted image of the great god Pan, the Greek god of nature, or of the Celtic Cɛ ɾunnos, the horned god of hunters and fertility of herds. What we touch upon here is that such primal images, met under meditative or imaginative circumstances in hallowed places, will inspire us to music. You don't have to be a trained musician; after all, none of the traditional folk or even medieval musicians was 'trained' in the modern sense, though they did preserve comprehensive disciplines of their own through oral tradition. To recapture this primal inspiration, we need take only a simple pipe, flute, flageolet or drum, or perhaps a simple stringed instrument.

Finally there is the implication, reaching back into medieval times, when the famous temple of Stonehenge was called 'The Giant's Dance' by chroniclers, that standing stones are petrified motion, frozen music, arrested dancers. This is deeply significant upon a mythic level: many such sites are aligned to stellar patterns and sightings, thus the dance of the stones reflects upon a geometric ground plan the dance of the stars. As discussed in Chapter 11, there are implications of music within the crystalline substance of standing stones that are supported by evidence from modern science.

# 5 Invoking Apollo

The universe is impelled by sound: Universal Sound is not mere noise, but an energy emitted by Original Being, which creates dynamic interchanges and polarizations, constantly proliferating towards material expression, and simultaneously reducing and withdrawing towards chaos, the void. This expression and withdrawal, itself being primal polarity, later generates harmonious relative patterns, which are traditionally called the Music of the Spheres. By the time this ceaseless interaction appears in the planetary or human world, it has again become sound, but as physical noise. Humanity, impelled by the spiritual impetus within, selects certain frequencies and patterns from the physical sounds, and affirms these to be music. Thus physical music is created out of physical noise, or harmony and polarity out of chaos: the outer world of nature holds within it the keys to the divine universal world.

Greek mythology defines chaos as the primal void, existent prior to the more personalized gods and goddesses; the Kabbala, which is the hidden tradition of the West, not confined to a Hebrew tradition but strongly represented by Jewish mysticism, calls the Ten Spheres, the Seven Rays or Seven Planets, the *Voices from the Void*. Similar concepts are affirmed in world mythology.[5]

Much has been said, and done, in modern attempts to state the music of the cosmos, the primal Sound. Many modernists and New Age musicians and composers attempt to approach the Original Sound, the cosmic music, through the use of formulae, mathematics, intellectualized patterns that are replicable upon computers. This is one approach, and by no means as modern and startling as we like to think. The ancient Pythagorean traditions, and the much later alchemy of the late Middle Ages and Renaissance, relied strongly upon what we would today regard as mathematical and computable (if not technically *computerized*) formulae.

Some artists and composers follow the ancient Hermetic tradition, in which the utterances of nature are said to mirror the utterance of Divinity. Perhaps the greatest modern master of this is the French composer Olivier Messiaen, who approaches cosmic music from an orthodox Catholic religion, yet with profound mystical insight rooted in the sounds of nature; sounds which are, or were for a long period of time, banned by the Catholic Church as being the voices of inherent paganism.

To approach the music of primal Being, we move away from human perceptions, and away from habitual modes of human conscious altogether as we currently understand them. The images of world religion and mythology, the mystical or magical practices of heightened or transformed awareness, all act as means to one end, reaching towards that ultimate perception. If we are truly able to hear the Music of the Spheres, we become transformed by it: we are never simply human again. This transformation is both beautiful and painful.

Western culture appears, superficially, to lack musical deities. I have cited Messiaen as a modern master not simply because of the profundity of his cosmic music, but because he has approached and gained inner perception of nature as a mirror of the Divine through a very orthodox religious tradition. The key words here are *approach through a tradition*: this is precisely why so many self-styled New Age musics are merely bland, commercial pop, for they are rooted in nothing but wishful thinking at best or blatant commercialism at worst. They have no deep spiritual, magical, or meditational tradition within or behind them.

Yet Christianity is, despite its traditions of religious art music, a most unmusical religion. It has no clear affirmation of music within its three major Images, God the Father, God the Son, and the Holy Spirit, though the Holy Spirit is *Ruach Elohim*, the ancient concept of the First Breath. The Feminine Deity was at one time Sophia, the Goddess of Wisdom, in the Gnostic Christian Trinity. She now appears as the Virgin, loosely disguising and enfolding all the goddesses of the ancient world into one uneasy image.

There is much to be gained by working with ancient gods and goddesses, using their forms concerned with music and musical inspiration. If we examine Western myth and religion, we suddenly find a quite comprehensive list of deities concerned with music and inspiration, even reaching through into early Christian saints, many in themselves restatements of pagan gods and goddesses.

In the ancient world music was closely, often inseparably, tied to both poetry and dance: hence deities of music were also powers of eloquence, movement, and of prophecy (which is a higher octave of poetry and not to be confused with idle fortune-telling).[6] We need only consider Norse, Celtic, and Greek traditions to immediately find some powerful images, both male and female, concerned with music. To explore these as sources of empowerment in modern meditation and musical inspiration, we can commence with the classical god Apollo, move away from him to the gods and goddesses of music in general, and then return to both Apollo and Orpheus, having found their antecedents and the often concealed aspects of their nature that link into the Mysteries of Light, which are also the Mysteries of Harmony. Although I have listed Apollo and Orpheus together, they are not always formally connected in ancient religion, though they have many images and motifs in common, and share a mythic relationship.

It is through such images, such interfaces, that our consciousness may approach the Music of the Spheres, and then the ultimate, infinite Sound of Being. Unless, of course, we take the perfectly valid and equally empowering path of orthodox religion, which has been defined repeatedly through the centuries in both East and West.

Apollo and the Greek traditions and myths connected to music are used as initial images due to general familiarity to many readers.

## Apollo, Orpheus, and Music

The earliest roots of Greek music, as in all world music, are mythic. This implies not only that they are so far back in time that no written records truly describe them but also that they are deeply embedded within the development of human culture, within the unconscious or primal ancestral levels of humanity. Scholars have frequently commented upon and compared aspects of Greek mythology with those of other European myths: the deepest levels, however, are comparable only in a mythic or poetical or archetypical sense, for they spring from the roots of human entity, and not from cultural exchanges, trade, conquest, or missionary work.

The mythic period of Greek culture dates from at least as early as the thirteenth century BC. The cosmic myth of the Argonauts is traditionally dated to this period (by the Ancient Greek historians), as is the musical hero or demigod Orpheus, who inspired the Argonauts with his music and song, and who developed a complex Mystery cult of his own. Other important early musical characters are Chiron the Centaur, musical teacher of Achilles, and Amphion.

At the simplest level Orpheus embodies the directly entrancing magical force of music expressed from the soul to the material world. His power is irresistible; it is also inseparable from poetry. The fundamental Orphic myth deals with musical enchantment, with ravishment that causes wild beasts to become tame, the forces of nature to become calm.

The raging furies are temporarily stilled by the music of Orpheus, which gains him admittance to the Underworld, to Hades, where he seeks his lover, Eurydice.

This myth offers us a very primal image of a god or mediator of music: Orpheus is the pure force of music to rebalance, to inspire, to inwardly harmonize those chaotic and natural forces which abound. The ultimate route that such inspiration takes is, inevitably, downwards to the Underworld, in pursuit of the ultimate balancing force to itself; this is represented by Eurydice. The fact that Orpheus does not succeed in bringing her back from the depths is a very profound insight into the nature of wild musical inspiration: it always leaves the Orphic mediator lonely, unsatisfied, and longing, even though he, or she, communicates great power and beauty to others. There is, however, a cosmic level, a higher octave to the Orphic myth, which is directly concerned with the universal creation. This universal power of beauty and inspiration, which created the worlds, is reflected through specific harmonics into the human poet or demigod Orpheus, so causing both his power and his agony.

Amphion is said to have used the power of sound to move rock, to build the great settlements of Cadmea and Thebes. His legend is therefore concerned with the potential harmonizing and structuring power of music, and reiterates a myth found repeatedly, that in ancient times direct physical effects, often upon a large scale, were gained through the use of music. The biblical version is, of course, the siege of Jericho, while in Celtic tradition we find that Merlin transported the Hanging Stones, Stonehenge, from distant Ireland, through the power of sound. Modern physics has now confirmed that the power of sound is indeed able to move, and to destroy, objects and life forms; and, more subtly, that matter itself has a musical resonance, the property of its atomic oscillation.

The main god of music and poetry (which were inseparable to the Greeks) was Phoebus Apollo. During one of the important cultural transformations of Ancient Greek society, Apollo seems to have replaced certain roles of the Great Goddess, and became the director of the Nine Muses. They in turn were communicators of the arts of music, poetry, dance, and cultural growth, through inspiration which gained specific form. Although Apollo is always associated with the lyre, it is important to remember that he did not invent it, for the lyre, or cithara, originated as a toy made by Hermes, the god of the questing intellect, the trickster mind, and the bearer of messages between worlds. Apollo is also referred to as Citharoedus, the lyre player, or Musagetes.

In Homer there is a very important description of Apollo as god of death, music, and healing. With this mythic fusion of what are, to the modern materialist mind, apparently antagonist forces, we find deep insights into the nature of Apollo and of music, vitality, and the life force. During battle, Apollo lets fly the arrows of death; yet his bowstring emits a musical tone as they are released, doubling or trebling its resonance or frequency. These overtones produce a healing sound, which cures wounds and eases the troubled mind. Such a myth is not merely heroic but touches upon the cosmic musical Mystery, as outlined in Plato's *Myth of Er* (see Appendix 3).

The modern image of Apollo is as a strictly male, rather severe image, the god of intellectual reason, manly arts, therapy, and the male image who, at an early time, slew the great Python of the Goddess at Delphi, and so took over her oracular shrine. This is a rather unfortunate image, deriving in many ways from the writings of Robert Graves, who would himself never have subscribed to later radical feminist interpretations of his poetical versions of Greek Myth.[7] But there are earlier, deeper variants of Apollo, where we find him to be not a rival to the Goddess but her beloved Son. This is the proper relationship between solar gods and the Great Mother: the Mother and the Son of Light.

Apollo was also known in the north and west of Europe, and the Greeks asserted that he had come from Hyperborea, a mysterious northern island often identified with Britain. The Etruscans had a god, Veiovis, who was similar to Apollo in many ways, and we find the image of a young god, concerned with light, healing, and music, the Son of the Mother, to be at the foundation of all of these and other variants. It is at this level that we might employ the image for modern visualization in connection with music and inspiration. Here too we find certain connections with the legend of Orpheus, and with the savage cult of Dionysus, which preserved in Greece the older primal traditions that had become greatly formalized within the worship of Apollo as a sun god.

In Celtic tradition, and in Romano-Celtic inscriptions which prove the historical existence of active worship, we find the divine Son called Mapon or Mabon. This simply means 'son'; he is referred to as Mabon son of Modron in Welsh legend, which simply means, 'Son of the Mother'. Although little remains of his formal cult, we find that his myth involves the cycle of all nature, a quest for a sacred child, and that he was patron of prophecy, poetry, and music. The Hyperborean Apollo referred to by the Greeks came from a triangular island with circular temples of stone, and every 19 years his people worshipped with the

Figure 3

# The Planetary Lyre

One of the earliest and most enduring models for the relationship between music, consciousness, and the universal creation, was that of the lyre. This is often taken to be a mythic conceit, or an 'allegory', but the use of the lyre was based upon precise attributes and harmonic patterns that are physical rather than allegorical.

Simple lyres are instruments with open (unstopped and unfretted) strings. Although the number of strings varied historically, a seven-stringed lyre was frequently associated with the relationship of the Sun and Planets, as in our illustration. The musical notes allocated in our example are based upon a simple modern scale of C major, but any relative mode or set of notes could be employed, and the relationships would still remain true.

The lyre (and similar instruments in ethnic music to the present day) is not limited to merely plucking of the open strings. Skilled players induce harmonics or overtones by lightly placing the tips of the fingers against a nodal-point on a string or strings, while plucking with the other hand. This technique brings out a very wide range of overtones and complex melodies and harmonies are possible using only seven open strings (or whatever small basic number is built into the instrument).

The diagram shows how a central harmonic, in this case the note F, represents the sun, with the Planets relating to this central utterance through a pattern of fundamental notes and harmonics.

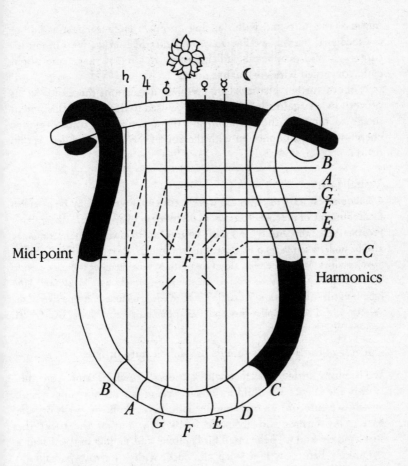

music of the harp and with dancing. In much later legends, as late as the medieval period, we find that the figure of Merlin, who began his career as child prophet, is still linked to this inner image, the bright child concerned with cosmic harmony.

Without further historical or mythical discussion, therefore, let us proceed to a visualization which may be used to draw upon this potent image to tap into the harmonizing, therapeutic, and transformative energies of music connected with the Son of the Mother, called Apollo or Mabon.

## Visualization

*Operational Notes:* For advanced work these visualizations may be preceded by the attuning of the six Directions, as described in Chapter 14. As the training programme for the Directions is fairly lengthy, the following visualization may also be undertaken in its own right, simply through relaxed use of the imaginative faculties. It may be read aloud to a group, each member taking a turn to do the reading, or may be studied on the page, simply as a story, and later rebuilt in silent meditation. A reading with music is included on side two of the cassette which accompanies this book, distributed by Sulis Music, BCM 3721, London WC1N 3XX.

*Opening music* The clear sounds of a simple harp or lyre.

We begin by sitting in silence with our eyes closed, breathing steadily. Within the silence we build an image, seeing it with our inner vision. Slowly we enter into a hot summer landscape, with the earth dry and bare. Tiny bushes and aromatic herbs grow out of the rocks that surround us, and we hear small birds piping and singing in the distance.

Directly before us is a steep cliff face, with a narrow passageway leading into a dark cleft in the rocks. The sun beats down, the small birds sing, and we smell the strong perfume of the herbs. There is no other sign of life.

From deep within the cleft in the rocks, we hear a faint sound of music, clear simple notes, which seem to come from far below. When they cease, we know that we must enter into this dark chasm, and seek whomever is within. As we approach the rocks, they tower over us, and the entrance is narrow. We squeeze painfully through, feeling that the rocks might crush us to death. As we pass within, the heat suddenly vanishes, and we are in the cool shade, with the light of a dark-blue sky far above us. As we look up at this light for the last time before plunging into the darkness, we see stars faintly shining, revealed to us by the depth of the chasm filtering the daylight.

Before us now is a jagged cavern mouth, roughly triangular in shape. All is still, silent, waiting. We pass into the cavern, and the light fades almost entirely. For a few moments we stumble upon a stony floor, tripping over rocks, until we feel the walls with our hands, and our eyes grow accustomed to dim grey light. The passageway leads downwards, and as we slowly make our way into the cavern our hands feel the walls, carved with deep spiralling shapes. We long to hear again that strange music to give us confidence in our quest, but there is instead the deep ancient silence of rocks and earth, broken only by the faint sound of our own footsteps.

As we reach deeper into the cave, we suddenly hear a faint sliding, rasping sound ahead of us, as if some large creature is moving in the shadows. Still touching the walls, feeling the deeply cut spiral patterns, we slowly move forward. We come at last to a point where the passage widens out, and here a screen or curtain is hung across our path. Beside this curtain is a torch burning, set into a cleft in the rock. By its light we see that the walls of the cave are filled with tiny crystals, and that the spiral carving stops just before the curtain, which is of rough wool, dyed in random colours.

All is very still and silent. The torch flickers and gives a dim red light. The woollen curtain, seeming like the rough work of a country loom, sways slightly in the tiny draught of the burning torch as it draws air in from far above. In this shadowy torch-lit stillness, we feel a strange terror; it begins as a tiny trembling of the feet, and rises up the legs and the spine rapidly. The hair upon our heads bristles, and a cold burning thrills through our flesh. Our heartbeat increases, and our eyes water. As this flow of energy passes through us, a tiny mouse suddenly scurries out of a hole by the burning torch, and scuttles up the woollen curtain. When the mouse reaches the top of the curtain, it swiftly gnaws through a thread, and the entire cloth falls, revealing what is beyond.

Directly before us rears a huge serpent, looking down upon us, and even as we flinch back, it slowly turns upon itself, and glides off into the depths below. For a moment we are too shocked to move, and then the flowing energy that passes across our skin and through our hair seems to pull us after the serpent. If we seek the Player of the Harp, we must descend into his secret place below.

We step through the thick folds of the rough woollen curtain, and find that the huge serpent has gone before us. Where it has passed, the walls are faintly luminous, and we follow, uncertain of where it will lead, yet knowing that there are no other passageways or routes to take except to turn and reascend, admitting failure in our quest.

The dimly luminous walls reveal tiny crystalline rocks, and streaks of brightly coloured minerals in vivid greens, reds, purples, and metallic rainbow hues. Faintly in the depths below, we hear the sound of falling water, which gradually grows louder as we approach. The sound increases to a constant roar, until we see at last a rushing waterfall that passes like a second curtain over the passageway, falling from the roof above into a deep cleft in the floor. This is lit by a smoking torch, set into a cleft in the rock, and so rapid is the flow of water that it draws the smoke downwards after it.

We cannot see beyond this waterfall, and have no way of knowing how wide the crack in the rock may be. As we pause, uncertain how to proceed beyond the roaring waters, they cease to fall for an instant, and we see far beyond a glow of red light in the distance. Then the waters renew with great force, and we realize that if we are to proceed we must leap through them, and trust that we land safely upon the other side.

So, amid the roaring of the falling waters, we draw in a deep breath and run at full speed towards the waterfall. We leap straight through its icy waters, over the deep cleft into the unknown shadows below, and land upon the other side. A smooth tunnel stretches away before, lit by a red glow that grows brighter as we approach. We feel a steady throbbing deep within the ground, gradually building until it surrounds us, and as we draw near to the light, we find that it radiates from a huge wall of flame rising from the floor of the passageway beneath our feet.

Before this third curtain, a wall of fire, we pause, and in silence make our deepest prayers to the Son of the Mother, whom we seek.

*A silent pause here*

As we wait in silence before the curtain of fire, we hear a single note, sounding steadily, from beyond the flames. Someone strikes upon a string, and the clear, vibrant note rings out until the flame curtain quivers. The flames move in resonance with the note, and we see patterns within them rising and falling with the peak and decay of the repeated single tone. Now the hidden musician plays a second note, a high unearthly overtone of the first, and the flames change shape into a regular and beautiful pattern, sculpted by the sound of that overtone. Now the hidden musician plays a higher overtone upon the same string, and the flames part into two, dividing into a perfect vertical lens-shape. The edges of this lens stream with patterned fire, swirling and radiating heat and light. As the last resonance of the high overtone fades, we quickly step through the Fire Gate into the unseen place beyond.

We find ourselves in a high chamber of rock, at the far end of which steam rises from within a pile of rocks. Over the unseen vent from which the steam issues, a tall bronze tripod stands, and upon that a deeply engraved bowl is set. Coiled round the rock, with its head resting by the foot of the tripod, is the giant serpent, which seems to sleep. The fire curtain behind us hisses and crackles, the steam rises, the serpent sleeps. Of the unseen musician there is no sight, nor sound, nor hint.

We see before us a smooth worn area of floor, and one by one sit to wait, looking upon the rising steam and the sleeping serpent. The heady fumes of that deep, secret place fill our minds, and visions swim before us. Out of the steam we see a deep, black, seething cloud, filled with flashes of colour. Into this cloud a single high note is uttered, causing it to part and assume shape. A second note, lower than the first, is uttered, and the shape separates into amorphous clouds. A third note, lower than the second, is uttered, and the clouds explode from within with light. A fourth note is uttered, and the explosions of light begin to move, weaving patterns around one another. A fifth note is uttered and they take shape as stars and planets in the depths of space. A sixth note is uttered, and we look upon one star with its attendant planets, our vision drawn to a planet of blue and green and rolling white colours. The lowest and seventh note is uttered, and we fall towards that planet from a terrible height, and our awareness pauses in stillness, in silence, at the moment of that fall.

*Here a passage of simple harp music is played, uttering Elemental patterns and tones*

We open our eyes to find ourselves in bright sunlight, in a forest glade, beside a bubbling spring. Seated upon a rock is a youth with long, tangled, golden hair. He plays upon a seven-stringed instrument, which seems to change shape as he strikes the strings. He plays with both hands, one hand plucking the strings and the other touching them lightly to create ghostly harmonics and overtones from within each prime note. As he plays the trees move, leaves burst forth, the spring bubbles, fish leap from the pool, and flowers open around his feet. His eyes are of ever-changing colour, each colour shining with a note from the instrument that he plays. Within the surrounding trees many animals are drawn to the glade, and they look upon us without fear. In the presence of the Son, and the sound of his music, we remain silent.

*Here a silent contemplation is made*

During our contemplation an animal or bird has come to each of us, and sits or stands beside us. This creature is the companion allotted to us by the Son of the Mother, the Harper who utters all creation with his music, from stars to crystals, and whose secret sound directs the orders of life and their relationships with one another. We look well upon our companion from another order of life, and when we look up to the rock by the spring, we discover that the Harper has silently departed.

Now the sun begins to set, and in the evening light the trees cast long shadows over the sacred glade. One by one the animals and birds depart into the night, and we too must leave and return to our outer world. We feel that our companion creature will be with us on future inner, visionary journeys, and remember it well, fixing its image and its qualities in our memory.

Slowly, peacefully, the inner light fades, and we find ourselves sitting in a familiar room. We sit in silent contemplation, and breathe steadily.

*The group makes notes, discusses, or simply disperses in its own time.*

# 6 Therapy, Emotions, Patterns

Music is increasingly used in therapy today, though any honest music therapist will admit that he or she cannot fully describe the underlying principles concerned. Modern music therapy may seem, superficially, to hark back to classical Greek and derivative medieval theories in which certain modes (scales) and rhythms have a known effect upon the energy of the human organism, but the bases of the ancient theory and of modern music therapy are, in fact, dissimilar.

In modern work undertaken with groups or individuals with varying types and degrees of disabilities, techniques are still being developed on an experimental basis. Modern music therapy works because music has an inherently therapeutic power, not because of any confirmed theory of music therapy or any insight into the therapeutic or transformative power itself. The current revival of music therapy, therefore, tends almost to act in a vacuum, cut off to a great extent from established mainstream therapies and unable or unwilling to relate to ancient theories concerning music.

Perhaps the most conscious use of music therapy is in Steiner schools or residential establishments, where very basic principles employing music as a soothing therapeutic medium are still regularly put into practice. These principles are derived from the esoteric instruction and spiritual system developed from ancient tradition by Rudolf Steiner, founder of the Anthroposophical Movement.

Let us examine some of the more obvious principles involved in music and its transformative effect. Before proceeding, we must reaffirm a very important point: the transformative effect of music may be positive or negative, good or bad. The same principles are involved, for example, in violent aggressive music that arouses belligerent reactions as are involved in harmonious music that arouses a comprehension or inner state of beauty and balance. The difference is merely one of relative patterns. We shall return repeatedly to this matter of pattern or shape, and for the moment will merely let it stand as a preliminary statement, to be developed further as we proceed.

Music is effective as a therapeutic agent because, under the right circumstances, it can realign patterns of emotion, structures of consciousness or psychic energy. In very simple terms, when we feel sad or confused, a harmonious, positive piece of music (and for the moment we will not define any specific parameters or examples) will attract our negative patterns (emotions or thought-forms) and carry them along into new locations or shapes. The words used here – *attract, carry, location, emotion* – all involve a sense of movement. Emotion is moving out of, or moving beyond. Music has the power to move us out of rigid or self-devouring negative states of consciousness. This works because the inherent patterns within the music, its musical shapes, resonate through the rigid or stale coagulation of our inner state, and realign it, pull it out of its rigidity, and draw the energy inherent within the negative condition out into a new form.

We may approach this concept in a number of different ways: in the ancient world the system of the Four Elements permeated all conceptual models (see Figure 1). Elemental balance or imbalance was thought to exist in the human being in the form of *humours*, which were energy patterns or, alternatively, actual subtle substances, energies or fluids within the body system, that corresponded to the metaphysical elements of Air, Fire, Water, and Earth. Thus a condition of imbalance, in which a person suffered from an excess of melancholy, one of the humours, was actually the manifestation of an Elemental imbalance.

This type of theory persisted in medicine into the nineteenth century, and is still found in traditional medicine worldwide. For our present purposes, however, we can dispose of the fluids, humours, or similar fluxes, fluids, essences, or substances often assumed in traditional medicines, and intentionally stay with the basic Elemental model. This may be restated with some effect in terms of modern music therapy, music and meditation, music and consciousness generally. To do so does not in any way obviate any modern developments concerning either physical health or the psyche: it should be, and can be, used as a supplementary or parallel system, with special reference to music and the vital energies and consciousness.

The process of attraction, resonance, and realignment also occurs in negative music, music with an unharmonious or deleterious, unhealthy effect. There are, of course, a wide range of such effects, positive and negative, and their interaction varies from person to person, group to group, situation to situation. In ancient musical traditions such effects were known to vary also from place to place, during the time cycles of the day, the month, the seasons. Such refinements are still found in a fragmented form in the great and complex ancient traditions of Indian classical music, but are generally ignored otherwise.

Negative music will reinforce and rigidify negative states of consciousness: a typical example is the obsessive repetition of heavy rock music, used to exclude all other perceptions. Music of this sort is often reinforced with negative imagery on album covers or in supporting posters, stage shows, and videos. There is, of course, a school of thought that suggests that such imagery and music is a valuable cathartic outlet, acting as a releasing agent for negative emotions, aggression, fears, and so forth. This entire function of negative music and related imagery has not been adequately explored, for the advances of technology and presentation have raced ahead so rapidly within the last 30 years that they outstrip any thoughtful assessment of their effect.

There is no doubt, however, that magical and spiritual traditions worldwide place a strong emphasis upon catharsis and catabolic or negative (breaking-down) agencies in consciousness. Modern spirituality, particularly New Age material, chooses to pretend that this aspect of spiritual development either does not exist or is not necessary; one of the typically enervating effects of this is that familiar cosy glow of pseudo-spirituality, an all-up-in-the-air wonderfulness that has no foundation, no inherent reality. So, it might be argued, does not negative music with vicious imagery act as an agency to bleed off unhealthy negativity and channel it in harmless directions?

It does indeed act as an agent to draw off negative emotions and psychic energy, and to channel them away, in most cases, from obvious expression. But it is by no means harmless. We need only ask ourselves, for example, where does the energy go? The answer to this odd question may be expressed in several different ways, though they all amount to a similar type of answer. The parameters of energy and consciousness are broadly defined in Chapters 9–14. The art of guided imagery, discussed in Chapters 4 and 5, suggests how negative music and imagery may actually drain energies into self-perpetuating, unhealthy inner worlds or imaginative structures. Negative or positive, the power is essentially the same, but its orientation, direction, and effect varies according to will. We need only consider normal physical health, in which the eliminatory system must be fit, to realize that all input, all sweetness, leads in time to overload and poison. This is as true upon psychic and spiritual levels as it is for the physical organism.

Music as a therapeutic potency acts through its inherent anabolic powers, certainly, but the catabolic effects of musical resonance and patterns are just as beneficial. There is a curious fact concerning the life span of orchestral conductors and their health: they have a remarkable tendency to live long and seldom be ill. This can be attributed not only to the alertness of the conductor's mind, for he or she is undertaking one of the most complex and demanding tasks known to humanity, but to the physical effect of musical energies upon the body. The resonance of music acts right through to a cellular level, and any development of music therapy for the future must examine this potentially healing or destroying fact.

If we confine our use of music therapy merely to calming the emotions or helping in self-affirmation, these being the two main areas enabled by general music therapy today, we are touching only upon a fragment of the potential. The key to defining an organic music therapy that is aligned for a whole entity, spirit, psyche, and body may be found in an Elemental world-view. There is no suggestion that an Elemental model is the only possible one; simply that it has, in various forms, stood the test of time and developing science, reappearing again and again in various expressions, schools of thought, and practical application.

# 7  Hearing Beyond Hearing

The word 'clairaudience' appeared, along with clairvoyance and other 'clair-' words, out of the spiritualist (perhaps more accurately described as spiritist) movement. The apparently French ambience of these contrived words may have served to give them a false gentility in the nineteenth century, and they reappear frequently in modern literature. Yet both clairvoyance and clairaudience are catch-all terms – 'clear seeing', 'clear hearing' – with many confused, inaccurate interpretations.

The terms *inner vision* and *inner hearing* may seem more apt to modern use, as they avoid many of the rather cosy and naïve notions attached to clairvoyance and spiritism. As is often the case, the older esoteric traditions defined inner vision and inner hearing in precise ways, with several distinct levels, techniques, and identifying qualities.

I have discussed clairvoyance and its relationship to seership and the Second Sight elsewhere,[8] but it is not always possible to separate the inner perceptions into neat categories, any more than it is to separate the outer senses within daily life. Our perceptions, inner or outer, are a holism, with the separate functions or senses combining with one another in very complex ways.

There are well-established techniques, however, designed to separate, reunify, and enhance the physical senses through meditation, visualization, and ritual. These may be proven in meditation or other practices with absolutely no esoteric or inner requirements or aims. Such separation and enhancement techniques were originally devised and refined for magical or spiritual ends, and have been used for thousands of years to redirect attention. The aim is first to gain skill in focusing awareness and directing it, then to use that skill to cross over the seemingly rigid barrier between outwardly directed attention and the inner dimensions of consciousness, energy, and imaginative forces.

Once we cross the threshold of consciousness, and begin reaching within, and therefore 'away' from the outer senses that we have learned, to a certain extent, to separate and control, we find that the blossoming of inner senses and perceptions becomes once again a holism, in which direct separation is often difficult.

Beyond this second level or inversion, which is not in itself too difficult to reach, there is a further threshold gained by separating and reattuning the *inner* senses or perceptions, just as has been previously done with the outer ones. This third level, reached by inner disciplines, is where true spiritual perception begins. It is far removed from popular or spiritist or channelling notions of clairvoyance and clairaudience.

Most of the techniques and indicators found in this book, or in any textbook on esoteric training, are concerned with events that occur on the second level. Traditional training, however, always includes the means to reach the third level (see Figures 5 and 6), usually embedded within those of the first and second levels, but often unperceived or unactivated for many years of training and effort.

Clairaudience was, and still is, loosely used to describe the faculty of hearing that which is not heard by the physical ear alone. At its crudest definition we have the rather juvenile notion of discarnate spirits, seen only by clairvoyants, talking to receptive persons, who hear them only by clairaudience, and all unperceived and unheard by anyone else present. This is of course nonsense, not only to the sceptical modern scientist, psychologist or rationalist, but to the trained occultist or initiate into esoteric arts and disciplines. It simply does not happen in that way. Let us examine some of the concepts and practices of hearing beyond hearing, or listening within, and then relate them to the art of music.

## To Develop Inner Listening

Perhaps the best place to start is with the perennial technique of inner listening, found in religion, meditation, and magical arts throughout history and in all world cultures in varying forms. The practice of inner listening leaps far beyond the superficial notions of 'clairaudience', for it seeks, in meditation, to hear the original sound of Being. If you wish to develop your potential of hearing and listening, this is both the first and last step to take. Paradoxically it is the first level of training, but reaches to the third level of spiritual perception.

Inner listening begins with Silence: traditional techniques are used to reduce the input and conditioned or habitual reactions to the outer world. This begins by reducing sight, through the simple action of closing your eyes. Once your eyes are closed, begin listening to the place in which you sit: there are definite zones of sound, which take relative form as concentric, intermingling spheres of auditory perception. The furthest off is outside the building, or, if you are outdoors, is upon an auditory horizon which establishes itself almost immediately; its sounds are usually the most indistinct, but may, through enhancement of listening in meditation, become startlingly clear.

The second sphere or zone of perception is a middle zone, occupying a region within that furthest horizon, and with sounds that are more distinct and readily heard. We are particularly aware of sounds of approaching and departing movement in this zone, and in normal perception such sounds are generally registered unconsciously long before the source of the sound becomes close enough to merit direct attention.

The third zone is personal and immediately around us. It has a variable spatial size, but is usually quite small. It encompasses sounds that directly affect us, and those which we ourselves make. In meditation, this immediate sphere can be deliberately reduced, and turned, so to speak, inside out. This exercise enables us to hear our physical inner sounds, such as breathing, pulse, heartbeat, and other sounds which are normally quite inaudible and unnoticed on a conscious level.

The auditory perception of the three interconnected zones is an invaluable exercise. It consists initially of truly listening, something which we seldom do. The awareness is extended and then withdrawn through the three zones, and the new horizons of understanding and auditory perception that may be gained by this exercise are often surprising, even revelatory. But the purpose is not simply to enhance hearing and begin real listening, important though such a redirection of habitual perceptions may be.

The zone exercise in physical listening is a physical operation only in the sense that it focuses awareness upon outer sounds; after some experience and skill has been gained, the same attention, concentration, and triple zoning of perception may be turned inwards in meditation. Without the preliminary training in *relative perception*, the individual is often lost upon the inner dimensions of his or own consciousness.

We pass within through the contemplation and Approach to Silence (see page 155), and immediately find that we have inverted or reflected the three zones of listening.

The first inner zone reveals inner sounds that begin where the minute body noises and resonances are lost. It corresponds to the spiral between the Earth and the Lunar World (see Figures 5 and 6), partaking of both to varying extents. Meditators worldwide report the phenomenon of a hissing silence, which can be deafeningly loud, yet totally still. It occurs during the first crossing of the inner threshold in meditational listening, and reoccurs on a much higher octave in the deepest meditation or contemplation. This is not a physical phenomenon, but a level of inner hearing. In traditional terminology it is called the Roaring Ocean. Another well-attested inner phenomenon is the babble of ceaseless voices; this particular threshold is also encountered just before going to sleep, and is usually interpreted by modern psychologists as a random replay of fragments from the unconscious mind breaking through before sleep proper.

In meditational traditions, the voices are sometimes known as those of the Ancestors, and there are a number of ancient techniques for attuning to specific voices through ancestral meditation. The Roaring Sea, Voices in the Valley, and River of Blood are all part of the second zone of inner hearing. In this middle zone, which corresponds to the spiral between the Lunar and Solar Worlds, partaking of both, most experiences of inner listening occur. It is here that we first perceive inner music, specific inner voices, and the innermost sounds that come unasked, bringing with them sudden realizations. This *last* category of sounds experienced by inner hearing breaks through from the third level, which spirals between the Solar and Stellar Worlds.

It is upon this third level that we truly hear the Music of the Spheres, which is a polyphonic or multifold set of relationships, using intervals that weave and elide within one another. The Music of the Spheres is, for us, the result of inner perception attuning to the resonances of energies and entities in the Solar System: the utterance of the Planets and the Sun in harmony with one another.

Though it may be heard by analogy and through imagination upon the second level of inner hearing, which is greatly enhanced by training exercises and Elemental patterns such as those included in Chapters 12 and 14, the Music of the Spheres truly belongs upon the third or deepest level of inner hearing. A simpler but more difficult approach to this universal level of hearing, listening to the entity that is our star and its worlds, is through long meditation in silence. Within this silence many sounds and visions eventually rise, but they too are stilled until the inmost resonance of Being is heard. It is upon this mystical path that the Music of the Spheres may be heard.

The Music of the Spheres is not a set of chords or harmonies, but a complex interaction of microtonal melodies. Sometimes the intervals are of great proportions, while frequently they are very small: in most cases the audible Music of the Spheres, heard upon the third level of inner hearing, involves a constant microtonal gliding and interweaving between a number of voices. The voices are those of the energies and entities (Sun, Moon, and Planets) of our Solar System. Beyond this choir is the music of the universe, the outer sounds of which may now be heard through modern astronomical and physical listening devices. The inner sound of the universe is heard through a profound change of consciousness in meditation. The microtonal nature of cosmic music has been reported by many seers and meditators, and may be followed through in the properties of acoustics as they appear in our own range of physical hearing.

Due to the paradox of expansion and contraction of certain intervals, and the metaphysical nature of the octave, various musical compromises have been devised for instrumental accord. These tempering systems allow small inaccuracies or variations between the intervals of nature and the intervals agreed upon in contrived use in instruments. The human ear can adjust within wide parameters, and is rather generous in letting us pass over variations in tuning. The ear seeks to find proportion and harmony, as can easily be shown by listening to a deliberately out-of-tune instrument. Within a short period of time we notice the inaccuracy no less, but have temporarily adjusted to it.

The whole issue of temperament, as it applies today, means that we cannot imitate or reflect the Music of the Spheres directly on modern instruments. Several composers and inventors have suggested ways of coping with this cyclical problem, including special instruments, varied types of temperament, and nowadays the totally programmable electronic synthesizer.

Ironically, the now defunct ethnic musics of the West contained microtonal intervals which were consciously employed by musicians and singers, just as they are in other world musics to this day. Such environmental music reflects, to a certain extent, planetary and solar music; but Western art and popular music, with its rigid reduction of the scale, cannot by its very nature produce certain intervals that seem to be of cosmic origin.

One method of surmounting this problem, used, interestingly, by both formal composers and by musicians who play by ear rather than by sight, is through interaction and overtones. When selected notes are sounded together, a variety of overtones occur, and by allowing natural resonances to build and interact with one another, many ghost intervals or overtones, even undertones, arise. These are properties of nature, and not of equal temperament. The human voice has similar overtone properties, and it is primarily the voice that is used in specialized musical empowerment and Elemental work, for this very reason.

# 8   Squares, Sigils, Sacred Dance

## Squares

Magical Squares and Sigils occur repeatedly in both esoteric literature and oral teaching tradition reaching from the earliest times to the present day. They are a subject shrouded in superstitious nonsense, with any sensible use deliberately confused and disguised for many reasons, both good and bad. Yet despite this unpromising scenario, magical squares and sigils remain part of the mainstream tradition in esoteric arts, though it must be admitted that they are generally taken on trust or in the spirit of crude experimentation and application, rather than in full understanding. There is a long underground tradition of applying magical squares to letters of the alphabet, thus generating sequences of words or names; this is partly derived from Hebrew tradition, where the concept of a divine originative alphabet is developed in mysticism and religion to a very high degree.

Hebrew tradition, however, is by no means our sole source of this important esoteric transformative or magical art, for the root concept of sacred letters or signs is found at the heart of religion and magic worldwide. The concept is also expressible, and frequently expressed, in terms of music.

Musical presentation may be the best possible form of communication and use of magical squares, for music is not dependent on cultural symbols or religious dogma. Magical squares and their musical meta-physical potential may also be examined in the light of recent math-ematical patterns expressible through computer models (such as the Mandelbrot sets); indeed, it is clear from such 'discoveries' in com-puterized visual models, based upon mathematical reiterations, that magic squares were and are exactly the same type of model as those now unconvincingly called 'chaos' models. These are, in short, holistic patterns that are inherent in what were long considered to be random or unacceptable sequences of numbers.

The sequences themselves describe or represent interactions of energy or events, and this leads to the rather odd situation where computers and prophecy hold an uneasy common ground, where neither technology nor seership utilizes concepts of statistics or linear cause and effect, but operate together upon quite different bases.

In short, magical squares are the remnant of a precise temple science in which specific sequences of numbers, sounds or symbols were reiterated in carefully defined cycles. This metaphysical or magical science is exactly mirrored by new physics and mathematics today, with holistic models that were not accessible to linear thinking until high-speed refined calculating machines appeared. The result? A simple restatement of certain cycles and patterns long established in spiritual and magical arts through the vehicles of disciplined imagination, harmonic resonance with the planetary environment, and the bioelectrical organism itself.

What computers do is to reaffirm ancient truth in a modern way, thus helping to destroy many of the crude fallacies and illusions of materialist reason and linear logic.

How can magical squares be applied in music, then, and how might they be used directly for inner transformation and empowerment?

The principle is very simple indeed, no matter how universally variable the outcome, and like the genetic code, it is based upon rotations of specific units in varying combinations. The Elemental model, which is at the heart of modern genetics no matter how much this might be denied by biologists or geneticists, generally unfolds from four principal *entities*, defined as letters or numbers.

In magical squares, number sequences are written out in a square or block, and may be read or activated in various directions once they have been allocated spatial form. This is an elusively simple but powerful concept; the abstract of *number* is given a *spatial* form, then a series of reiterations or rearrangements is found within that spatial expression. This is nothing more nor less than the act of universal creation in miniature; no modern physicist would deny such a statement, though it is central to the mystical and magical traditions rather than to materialist sciences.

## Sigils

In the inner traditions, such as were taught in the ancient temples and were perpetuated in a diffuse form by oral tradition well into the orthodox Christian era in Europe, specific squares of numbers were connected to certain planets, entities, and energies. Thus there are a number of confused works on ritual magic, mysticism, spirit conversation, and so forth which show Squares and Sigils for specific forces and forms. The Sigil is really a variant of the Square, for while the

Square shows lines of numbers within a spatial pattern which may be read or used in several orders, directions, or routes (see Figure 3), the Sigil is a graph or map of the routes taken, without the actual ground plan itself.

In most cases Sigils have become more corrupt than Squares in general publication and tuition, for they have long since been divorced from their ground plans, which were frequently communicated only in oral tuition. So Sigils have been corrupted through blind copying, fantastical application and extrapolation, and, of course, sheer ignorance. Many Sigils in publication today are merely crude copies or variations on proper symbols and alphabets, easily recognizable as derivatives or pieces of spurious mystification rather than examples of an exact art.

## Sacred Dance

The ultimate potential of this obscure but by no means lost art lies in the fusion of music and movement: sacred dance. We know from the profound traditions of India and other Eastern sources that temple dancing was not merely an act of worship, but a physical reiteration and re-creation of cosmic forces, mirrored with the human body moving to specific music in specific patterns. Similar traditions existed in the West, but the orthodox Christian Church made haste to ban dancing in connection with worship at a very early date, as it was central to pagan rituals, and a potent source of spiritual liberation. There are a number of references from classical sources which suggest that mime and dance held a powerful role in the mythic and religious expression of the ancient world.[9] The art remains today in various ritual dances preserved in folk traditions in the West.[6] This fusion of music and movement is so important that it commands fresh attention with each century; it is the human expression of the Magic Square, the Sigil, and the empowered musical pattern.

There is a general impression, much perpetuated by fiction and film, that ancient temple dance was of an erotic or 'Bacchic' nature, in which wild energies caused the dancers to fling themselves around in an abandoned manner, invoking ever-increasing sexual or emotional forces towards an orgiastic culmination.

This viewpoint is open to severe criticism, and is in fact a very modern and, in psychological terms, repressed fantasy involving the apparently lost rituals of the ancient world. The true nature of Bacchic and Erotic dance is found in the function of the mythic or divine beings and forces from whom it is named. Eros in a classical sense is quite different from the modern application of the term *erotic*, for Eros was the primal force

Figure 4

# The Four Energy Centres and Four Elements

The Four Elements correspond to and harmonically resonate within various energy centres in the human organism. There are a variety of both Western and Eastern esoteric, philosophical, and medical systems defining such energy centres. The number defined and used for practical work varies. The simple foundation to this theory and practice is, however, found worldwide. The human organism is understood to correspond to and resonate through various modes or levels of energy. These in turn are found within the Three Worlds (5) and to harmonically relate to the Lunar, Solar, and Stellar relative worlds or entities. The Lunar World is centred upon our planet Earth and the Moon, our own physical environment. The Solar World includes the Lunar World, the Planets and centres upon the Sun. The Stellar World includes the Solar World, and consists of our Galaxy, and ultimately the universe. All of this is mirrored in the human entity, the microcosm mirroring or harmonically reiterating the macrocosm.

An initial practical application of this conceptual model, based upon the human being standing upright upon the surface of the planet, relates the Four Elements to Four Zones or power centres. These are EARTH–FEET, WATER–GENITALS, FIRE–HEART, AIR–THROAT. The Octave or next spiral is within or slightly above the head, and is often attributed to SPIRIT. This is a higher octave of EARTH, and if a fundamental earth-tone of C1 is allocated to the zone of the feet, this highest tone would be C29, an octave of octaves above (see Figure 2). For practical purposes, however, these cycles of pitch and overtones are defined only as the fundamental Four Elements, giving the notes of CDEF(G) or 1234(5).

Practical chanting can be developed by focusing awareness upon an Element and a Power Centre. Exercises of this type are found in Chapters 12–14.

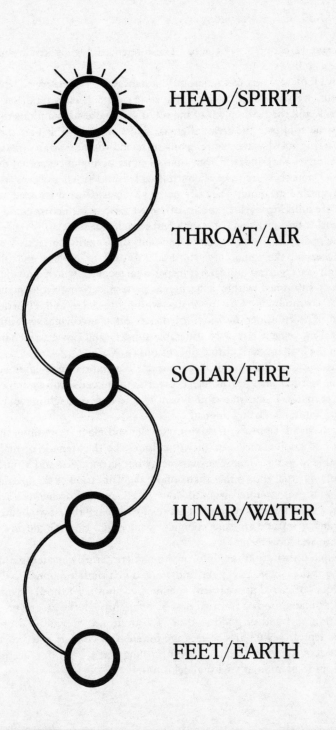

HEAD/SPIRIT

THROAT/AIR

SOLAR/FIRE

LUNAR/WATER

FEET/EARTH

that caused creation out of Chaos.[5] The difference is highlighted in ritual dance as follows.

If we look at living examples, at folk dances which preserve a ritual element, we will find that they have a very formal, even rigid, set of patterns, and that to step out of the traditional patterns is unthinkable. The same applies in the great religious dances of India, which are often inseparably fused with epic religious texts and their associated music. The energies may indeed, from time to time, be blatantly sexual and aroused, but they are always controlled, fed into ritual patterns, and given specific meaning. They are never idly wasted or dissipated and there are differing levels or modes of sacred dance which correspond to the worlds or dimensions of energy and consciousness.

The sexual or 'erotic' mode corresponds to, or more correctly *resonates within*, the Lunar and sub-Lunar World of Nature and pro-creation (see Figures 5 and 6). A transpersonal mode, in which individual entity is subsumed within a harmonic pattern deriving from higher orders, corresponds to or resonates within the Solar and Planetary World. The true hieratic mode of dance, often involving very little physical movement but of considerable subtlety and power, resonates within the Stellar and Spiritual dimensions or World.

This harmonic (hierarchical) approach to sacred dance is employed to bring spiritual energies through the worlds to indwell in full awareness in the sexual or Lunar state and dimensions, to flow through the sexual energy of a human being or group.

The basis of Tantra in Eastern mysticism and magic rests upon this premise. Temple dancers in ancient cultures, be they female or male, were able to arouse intense sexual energy but harmonized and attuned towards spiritual ends rather than temporal gratification or dissipation. They were trained intensively to draw upon spiritual archetypes and forces, giving them outer physical expression through their own bodies, and transferring and arousing energies within others through the power of music and movement.

Temple prostitution (an unfortunate modern term) was an essential feature of the Goddess religion, and worked in a similar manner to the techniques of sacred dance briefly summarized above. The body became a direct inhabitation of spiritual power, often through the archetype or mediation of a god or goddess form. Prostitution is a negative word, for the temple sexual arts were quite different in content and aim to the modern Christianized practice of selling one's body for fleeting gratification of another's sensual delusions.

# Communication

Magical squares and Sigils were also used for communication between worlds, between dimensions and different types of entity. Certain Squares and Sigils, such as those employed by John Dee in his *De Heptarchia Mystica*[10] and other profound works produced during the sixteenth to seventeenth centuries, were communicated by otherworldly beings. Thus we have an interesting concept, in Dee's work and frequently in the less well-publicized works of other esoteric researchers, by which codes or interdimensional languages and symbols are employed as a central part of the magical process. If we demystify this subject, it simply means that mathematics, pattern, and proportions form the basis of universal relationships, from the atomic level to the stellar, from the microbe to man to the archangel or stellar Being. Such shapes, such patterns, therefore, may be used for communication.

In Elemental and empowered music, we use the musical shapes to act as interfaces for energy (this is, of course, another way of describing communication). In general practice the communication is between levels or harmonics of our own entity and energies, such levels being defined by the Elemental system, and represented upon glyphs such as the Circle or Tree of Life. We use empowered music to alter the rate of rotation and emanation of our inner energies, and eventually to fuse these energies together as one harmonized Being.

But in the early stages of training, we are literally using music to communicate within ourselves, for it reaches areas of energy and consciousness within us that our conditioned behaviour and sluggish inner patterns normally bar from willed access. More simply, Elemental music is used to reunify and activate the Elements within us that have become imbalanced.

This is the (constructive and beneficial) polar opposite of being inspired by music: in general orchestral works, or religious music, we reach heights of perception and elation that are usually closed to us. The combined effect of the physical sound, its patterns, timbres, and the skill of performance, communicate to us something of the inspiration of the composer or the religion itself. But this is a temporary high: it does not necessarily reattune our own musical Elements and energies, or permanently raise perception and vitality. As discussed earlier (see page 63), music may also be used to degenerate and imprison consciousness and vital energies. Fortunately this too is an ephemeral effect, though we seem forced to admit that the degree of repetition of negative music in our cultures is far greater than the repetition of positive music. Let us now move on to methods of relating our inner energies harmoniously.

# 9    Voices From the Void: Cosmology, Music, the Tree of Life

There are various models used in esoteric, magical, and spiritual disciplines. They are essentially patterns which show microcosm and macrocosm, the human being and the universal being. They also reveal a harmonic, which is to say *musical*, relationship between all worlds, all entities. This harmonic property is one of the few true laws of matter/energy. We may employ a model based upon the reflection of light, in which mirrors or lenses polarize reflections and images in certain specific ways; we may also employ an acoustic model in which proportional relationships of sound, musical shapes, resonance patterns, also reflect, polarize, and mirror in specific ways. The law of proportion and reflection operates through all media, all relative states of energy and matter, from atoms to stars, from microbes to human consciousness.

In this chapter we shall be exploring a number of musical topics resonating around the central master-symbol of the *Tree of Life*, which shows the universal relative patterns of proportion, polarity, and reflection clearly and simply. This is not a detailed chapter of tuition or exposition of the Tree, for such material exists in abundance elsewhere; in some sections we shall appear to travel away from the central symbol of the Tree itself into discussions of the effects of music upon humanity today, and then return to the central symbol, and discover the relevance of the departure.

The aim will be to make the discussion of music and its effect upon consciousness as accessible as possible; to this end the Tree of Life is a very helpful device, as friendly to the reader who has no experience of its use as to the student who has already worked with it in meditation or visualization. Furthermore, as the Tree incorporates an ancient cosmological teaching that the universe was uttered as music, it helps us to attune to those perennial traditions of the ancient world which are now commanding such intense interest after several centuries of underground existence.

The Tree of Life is a harmonic model that reaches, in most versions though not in all, in ten interacting spheres or modes of energy and consciousness, from originative Being to expressed physical matter and biological life forms. It is reflected in the esoteric traditional constitution of humankind, in which the human body mirrors the body of the universe. Much of the empowering potential of music is said to be derived from its effect upon the various 'bodies' of humankind: the physical, the bioelectrical, the mental, the emotional, the spiritual. The Tree of Life defines these spheres of energy or bodies, and shows how they are, in fact, proportions of one entity. This concept is in itself inherently musical.

In the *Sepher Yetzirah*, one of the main early texts embodying the European Jewish mystical tradition of the Tree of Life, the spheres or *Sephiroth* are called '*The Voices from the Void*'. These Voices are uttered from the Void, from primal Chaos, and, arising out of the First Breath, rapidly develop into a harmonic pattern. Traditionally each Sphere or Voice is associated with a Planet of the Solar System. A translation of the text is found at the end of this chapter.

The Tree of Life is, therefore, a structure or glyph showing the musical relationship between the Voices or Music of the Spheres. It is an eminently musical structure, for it shows harmonic reflections and inversions, establishing a set of relationships similar to those found in acoustics, and more specifically in musical sound patterns.

There are many expositions of the Tree of Life, ranging from written and oral teaching, deeply rooted in genuine Jewish mysticism, to pan-cultural Renaissance expansions, a process which has persisted right into the present day with modern magical and meditational texts. They all vary in a number of ways, without ever moving far from the inherent harmonic structure of the Tree of Life itself. The secret of using a master glyph, a universal harmonic open-ended symbol or model, is that we should not be too rigid or dogmatic in our interpretation. Just as the universe is open-ended, a spiralling expansion and simultaneous contraction as revealed by logarithmic spirals found in nature, so is the Tree of Life.

Within defined but open-ended resonant parameters, symbolized as the Spheres, Voices, Planets, Worlds, there are many ways of interpreting and allocating symbols upon the Tree of Life. The musical suggestions which follow are intended as guides for meditation, visualization, and work with empowering music or chant. They are not proposed as dogma or the sole musical theory possible relative to the Tree.

## Music, Human Consciousness, and the Tree of Life

Before the new physics broke innocently into the realm of ancient wisdom teachings, there were various modern esoteric musical theories that attempted to find either a mechanistic model for music and consciousness, or applied an artistic or inspirational basis for the use of music to transform awareness. Although specific rates of vibration (the mechanistic model) and generally reapplicable emotional stimuli (the artistic model) are undeniably present in music, and are employed to give known or prerequisite results, neither of these form the basis for the perennial esoteric mystical or magical traditions of musical empowerment and harmony. The mechanistic and artistic effects of music, and any rules or observations applicable to them, are merely side effects. This statement is so important that is worth repeating in more precise terms: the emotional or biorhythmic responses to set musical patterns are lesser harmonics, side effects, and not major examples of music power.

The Tree of Life indicates relationships between various worlds or levels, and models such as the Tree have been used in esoteric training for thousands of years. We may, therefore, turn to such traditions in the knowledge not merely that they have been in operation for a long period of time but that they have proven their worth in the lives and training of many students. If this were not so, they would have vanished from use, rather than permeate both the underground and the orthodox spiritual and imaginative artistic traditions in so many ways.

Most important is the cosmic resonance, the tradition that the esoteric symbols such as the Tree of Life, the Axis Mundi, the Wheel of Life, the Zodiac, all define in varying ways as an actual universal entity, the cosmic body. In other words, as they are broad, open-ended symbols of multi-dimensional reality, they speak to our intuition, they regenerate freely and cannot be suppressed or corrupted.

The Tree of Life is shown in Figure 5, with particular regard to music rather than its many mystical and magical ramifications. The reader will find this illustration helpful during the following discussion, and ultimately it is intended as an image for meditation and contemplation, linked to specific empowering tones. The Tree of Life is not merely a reference illustration, but a practical and highly concentrated, powerful key image that opens into further and further levels of realization, inspiration, and enlightenment. For those who are already familiar with the Tree of Life, the musical suggestions offered here may form an additional aspect of their existing work.

## Music and Feeling or Emotions

It is well known that music arouses and directs the emotions: Plato said as much in *The Republic* when he described the effect of certain modes or scales upon the ardour of young men and the characteristics of modes evolved through regional or racial consciousness. In a gross sense music is used constantly today to rouse ephemeral, spurious, even negative emotion, for commercial and political reasons. Upon this level, the basic emotional and elemental theories of Plato or Pythagoras still apply to us at the close of the twentieth century, though the details of scales and rhythms, and the technical apparatus of making music, are very different indeed from those of the Ancient Greeks.

Let us examine some of the processes that appear to operate when we listen to music (the term *appear* is used intentionally at this stage, as the operation of music within consciousness is by no means limited to 'cause and effect'). Typically obvious cause and effect in music is usually of the self-reinforcing feedback type, in which a rigid or circular inner condition (an emotional pattern or state) is fed, and in turn feeds energy into a specific, limited, closed type of music.

Such feedback, of the sexual/emotional sort (though acoustic feedback is also a typical device used almost as a hallmark of heavy rock music), is clear in commercial popular music, and is unquestionably used in other artificial constructs to enclose and separate the audience or recipient from any other source of stimulation or awareness. Such a suggestion is by no means one of artistic élitism or indeed of any type of *artistic* criticism, but of simple fact. Furthermore, audiences, when questioned, readily confirm that in certain popular musics, heavy rock being a main example though there are many more, the aim of the record, concert or experience is precisely to shut out the world.

The popularity of the Walkman tape-recorder and radio affirms this intent for the individual: this device is able to produce ear-damaging volume in (almost) totally exclusive individual intimacy; the ultimate in modern musical masturbation. The group or concert experience, however, depends on the physical vibrations of very high levels of noise, acting not only through the hearing upon the emotions and imagination, but upon the entire physical and psychic organism.

But surely, we might say, this exclusion of the world is part of the mystical or spiritual process. Do not wise men and women retire into silent lonely places and practise meditation? Is there not sacred music designed to shut out gross levels of existence and lead the emotions into higher realms? Well, this has frequently been stated, but it is by no means a true or full picture. The ascetic or even the ordinary day-today meditator does indeed shut out the distraction and trivia of mind and body habits, the constant rattle, roar, and whine of a noise-polluted culture. The monastic or the spiritually inspired listener does indeed prefer the pure tones of Gregorian chant, say, to those of the pre-programmed synthesizer playing pop music. But in both cases they seek, or should be seeking, openings and openness to the real world, the world of land, planet, solar system, to expand their listening consciousness through chosen channels that lead into a greater understanding.

The esoteric techniques of spiritual music are designed exactly with regard to one end: they lead into a higher consciousness which is inclusive, open, holistic. This is the true higher consciousness, rather than the demonic illusion of élitism, the dogmatic or tempting 'higher spirituality' found in many world religions and in various sects and cults which despise, reject, and neglect all non-members, all of the world, merely to reinforce their own superiority.

So we have repetitive popular music which seeks to enclose and reinforce, to feedback, while the perennial traditions of consciousness in music seek to open out. Both use similar techniques, both aim at first to shut out the customary world. But the main aims, and the pathways, and the use of inner power, are very different indeed.

One matter of concern to the present writer, and to many others involved in the arts and disciplines of the imagination, is the increasing use of both gross and subtle negative music techniques and examples in classes, books, courses, and recordings, which declare themselves to be 'spiritual' or 'New Age'. Many of the writers, teachers, composers, and recording artists who perpetrate such music today were introduced to it in the 1960s, when consciousness was changed by the use of acid, LSD, while listening to heavy rock or related consciousness degrading closed-system musics.

Today recording artists can be demonstrated historically and musicologically to be drawing upon the customs of music-making established in that naïve but dangerous period when realms of the imagination were being crudely explored by more people, in Western culture, than at any time since the sixteenth century in Europe. The actual taking of LSD is no longer relevant to the development of certain streams of modern popular music which emerged from the use of this drug in the 1960s; such musical streams have now established several well-defined vehicles and forms.

What, the reader may ask, has this attack upon Rockers, Hippies, and New Agers to do with the Tree of Life? The Tree helps us to define where energy comes from, and where it goes. The problem with closed-circuit or feedback music is that while it succeeds in its stated aim, that of shutting out or temporarily suspending awareness of the regular, admittedly corrupt, world, it leads nowhere. Indeed, it has a very pernicious effect, for it drains energy away into resonances, areas, modes – *worlds* in the ancient terminology – which are distinctly unhealthy for humanity. The crude symbolism of Pomp Rock and Heavy Metal shows this negative aspect in childish but clear forms; the subtle, repetitive, lulling, synthesized monotones of New Age music have a very similar effect, but using a different overt set of aims and symbols. Some of the problems of using synthesizers for meditative or transformative music are discussed in Appendix 2.

## The Tree of Life

To approach music in the context of the universal relationships and proportions shown on the Tree of Life, we may separate certain sets of relationships for working purposes. In reality they interpenetrate one another, and the use of separate lists is merely a convenience for initial reading and for clarity of the printed page. Our first set shows the expansion and expression of music, and may be applied either to individual works, to entire musical traditions, or to special empowering techniques such as Elemental chant, plainsong, or mantrams. It moves inward, from expressed sound to origination of Being (see Figure 5).

10. Physical sound: expression of Four Elements as audible music
9. Fusion of 1–8 as musical entity: biopsychic power of music, musical traditions, potency of tones and vowels
8. Intellectual power/   stimulus and structure of music
7. Emotional power/   stimulus and transmission of music
6. Central relationship or holism of musical entities, fusion of 1–5 as proportions of harmony
5. Laws of limitation (contraction of octaves)
4. Laws of expansion (spiral of fifths)
3. Relationship (through octaves) within universal form
2. Relationship (through octaves) within universal energy
1. Origin of Being: First Breath: Archetype of Four Powers
0. Unattainable Silence

Our second set moves through three spirals or levels of harmonic relationship, showing how universal energy/form is reflected into expressed music (see Figure 5).

1–3: 1 Being/   2 Universal Form/   3 Universal Energy. First Triad
4–6: 4 Expansion/   5 Restriction/   6 Central Balance or Harmony. Second Triad
7–9: 7 Emotion/   8 Intellect/   9 Psychic unity or fusion. Third Triad
10:  Expression as audible sound in musical proportions

Our third set shows the traditional planetary and primal magical or mystical attributes of the Tree of Life, which should be compared in meditation to those listed in the first two sets.

1. Primum Mobile (First Breath of Movement of Universal Being)
2. The Zodiac: the Star Father/   Wisdom (Stars or energy uttered into space and time)
3. Saturn/   The Great Mother/   Understanding
4. Jupiter/   The Giver or Vitalizer/   Mercy
5. Mars/   The Taker or Destroyer (originally a Goddess image)
6. Sun/   Harmony/   Illumination/   The   Child   of   Light/   Beauty
7. Venus/   Emotions/   Victory
8. Mercury/   Thought (Intellect)/   Honour
9. Moon/   Foundation/   Sexuality and collective consciousness
10. Earth. The World of Matter and its inhabiting entities, which partakes of and expresses all of the above, from a universal to a planetary scale.

There are a number of ways of defining musical patterns and intervals on the Tree of Life, and these may be assessed only by their practical effect. The ancient cosmologists, working from a geocentric system, conceived of the universe as a series of concentric spheres (shown as rings in most illustrations). A note or utterance was allocated to each ring and its inhabitants: planets, stars, angels, and other entities. The Earth was shown at the centre.

A heliocentric system revealed certain polyphonic proportions as properties of shape, of dimension, of geometry. This concept was both seen in a visionary manner and correctly calculated by Johannes Kepler in the late sixteenth and early seventeenth centuries. It seems to dispose of the old single note per sphere or circle geocentric system, particularly as it enabled scientists to calculate orbits and define the nature of the solar system as we know it today: with the planets in orbit around the Sun.

There is, however, still an important case to be made for the geocentric

Figure 5

# The Tree of Life

The Tree of Life is a pan-cultural symbol, found in various forms
throughout the world. Many modern versions of the Tree of Life are
published in English, and there has been a constant organic refinement
of the symbol for several centuries.

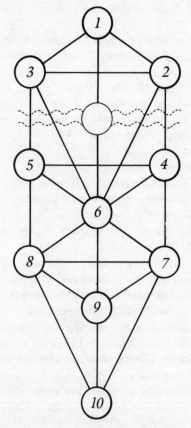

1) Original Source of Being out of Non-Being. The first breath of
   the universe, the seed of consciousness and energy. The CROWN
   of the Tree of Life.
2) WISDOM: primal power in motion. Associated with active
   analytic 'male' divine energy. The utterance of the Word or
   Worlds.

3)  UNDERSTANDING: primal vessel that contains power.
    Associated with catalytic receptive 'female' divine energy. The
    Great Mother.

4)  MERCY (The Giver): a reflection or harmonic of (2) in which
    the energies of creation issue across the Abyss. The positive
    anabolic male power of giving-out. The building force of creation.

5)  SEVERITY (The Taker): harmonic vessel of (3). Catabolic,
    receptive, female. Represented in traditions worldwide by a severe
    female divinity. The cosmic destroying force, breaking down and
    purifying.

6)  CENTRALITY or BEAUTY or HARMONY: balanced fusion of
    all energies. A hermaphrodite or bi-sexual power which reflects
    the Crown and acts as the central focus for all energies below the
    Abyss which separates the upper Triad (1/2/3) from the
    remainder of the Tree. Traditionally this is the realm of the
    Saviour, the Sons of Light, the Divine Kings. It also represents
    the Sun of our solar system.

7)  VICTORY: the Young Goddess or Flower Maiden. The
    emotions. An anabolic active female sphere. Associated with
    Venus traditionally.

8)  HONOUR: the young god. The intellect. A catabolic receptive
    male power. Both Honour and Victory exchange polarities.
    Associated with Hermes.

9)  FOUNDATION: male and female united. The matrix of
    expressed life forms and materialized energy; all previous Spheres
    fuse together. Associated with the Moon goddesses and gods.

10) KINGDOM: the expressed world drawn from all of the foregoing.
    Paradoxically this world is closest to the CROWN.


## THREE PILLARS DEFINED

There are Three Pillars or polarizations overall; left, right, centre. The
Central Pillar (which is the spindle of the sphere of the universe) is
neutral, bi-sexual or balanced. The left-hand Pillar is feminine and
catabolic, while the right-hand is masculine and anabolic. There is an
overall rotation from bottom centre (10) through 8/5/3/1 and returning
1/2/4/7 to 10. This cycle turns upon the pivot of 6.

A second rotation is found between left and right (2–3/4–5/7–8) while
a third rotation is found between the Crown and the Kingdom or Being
and Matter. These three conceptual rotations lock together to form the
overall Sphere of Being.

models, though not, I hasten to add, in the sense of the Earth being the literal centre of the solar system or universe. The true value of the geocentric model lies in its relationship to awareness: the central point, the unattainable locus of Being is in the heart of humanity upon the planet Earth – at least, as far as we are concerned. In meditation, the individual is at the centre of all Being.

Upon a higher octave (several higher octaves in fact) we find the Sun as an entity, a Being, at the centre of its planetary and energy system. This star is also the centre of the universe, as far as its own entity is concerned. Upon a higher octave again, we find the Galactic Zones and their centre. The concept that is maintained throughout is a *centric* one: proportions are defined through relative positions and patterns; the inner centre of Being is wherever awareness pauses and reflects, reaching into Stillness or Silence.

As far as empowerment through music is concerned, we need to find patterns and cycles that arouse Elemental energies through the various worlds or levels or spirals of the Tree of Life. These are found as energy centres (*chakras*) within the human body. Through the universal law of octaves and harmonics, utterance of empowered tones and musical shapes will arouse, amplify, and transform the forces inherent within the human entity.

What all of the foregoing comes down to is this: it does not necessarily matter which musical notes we allocate to a universal glyph such as the Tree of Life or the Circle of the Four Elements; what matters is that we find a relative set of pitches and patterns and extend them through the Worlds. The inherent nature of the universe does the rest, provided we truly utilize our own psychic-sexual energies (i.e. the body, the sexuality, the emotions, the intellect, the imaginative faculties, and so forth), all of which may be separated as a word list on paper, but in truth interact within one another as a holism.

There is considerable value is defining the audible octaves of the planetary and solar tones: these frequencies are of great importance to us as life forms within the solar system, and give levels or thresholds of relative pitch for empowered music.[11] But transformation through inner disciplines must be more than reattunement to the planets or the sun: these are starting-points, our cosmic status, so to speak. Besides, we are constantly cut off from these frequencies by our artificial pitching of modern music, now standardizing at A = 445 whereas only a few years ago it was A = 440 cps, which is in itself sharp to planetary pitch cycle, which begins around a low C, flat to the modern C on a keyboard, but found in ethnic musics as a pitch standard.

This is where the use of empowered tone, vowel utterance, mantrams, and specific calls or *shapes* comes into magical and spiritual traditions. These musical entities, uttered either by instrument or more specifically by the human voice during altered states of consciousness, draw with and through themselves Elemental forces. By the law of octaves which permeates the universe, the Elemental forces of our world are the spiritual forces of Universal Being. For practical purposes there is a 'hierarchical', or more accurately a *harmonic*, spiral between the human entity and divinity. This is the old concentric circular glyph known to the Renaissance adepts, and drawn from perennial tradition reaching back thousands of years. It was not truly a crude rule of thumb with one note to each rigid crystalline sphere or iron ring, though this limiting and devalued version of the cosmic vision was promulgated by political Christianity.

In the system developed in this book (the foundations of which were first published in my book *Music and the Elemental Psyche*[1]), it is the modality or variation of four simple Elemental Calls as they pass through the spirals or Worlds that gives empowerment.

We can pursue the relationships between music, energy, and the human psyche upon the Tree of Life a little further.

Listening to music moves (*emotes*) our energies; it stirs us out of our grooves and repetitive cycles. It gives us an influx of certain Elemental forces that push us into a new spiral of inner and outer activity. Emotions and thoughts are carried upon the vehicle of the music, and new horizons are opened to our imagination and perception, often where the conscious mind was previously unable to break free of a repetitive cycle of entrapment.

In this important context music may be broadly categorized according to the ten Spheres of the Tree of Life (see Figure 5):

1.  Spiritual or inspired clear tones and chant
2.  Universal music uttered by the stars (now made audible to us through modern technology)
3.  Music of sorrow
4.  Music of compassion and hope
5.  Vigorous (martial) and thrilling music that rouses the listener to action
6.  Harmonious and balanced music that inspires a sense of proportion and beauty
7.  Emotional or romantic music that causes feelings of sensual love and of closeness to the sensuous qualities of nature

8. Rapid-moving, finely structured music, very often intellectual or avant-garde according to the standards of its own cultural period
9. Dream music, sexual music, arousing energies and perceptions that are usually unconscious. May also apply to collective or ethnic music, and so crosses through into expression as . . . .
10. The total range of physical sound. Often expressed musically (in art music) as patriotic or grand and materially inspiring music. Also ethnic or regional music that reflects the land of its origin strongly.

Each of the foregoing broad classifications has its negative or unhealthy inversion.

1. Unfocused, undirected, random utterances
2. Chaotic noise
3. Introverted and self-devouring music
4. Lush, overblown, gushing music
5. Militaristic and vicious music
6. Intentionally discordant and profoundly irritating music
7. Degenerate music that attunes the imagination to depraved sensuous experiences
8. Music without any soul: mathematically generated music or composed solely from a system, either in the composer's mind or from a machine such as a computer
9. Unfocused, random music that seeks to carry the psyche on pointless trips through undefined realms of fantastical semi-consciousness
10. Loud, repetitive music with intrusive, stereotypical structures and rhythms

We may now quote from and briefly interpret a traditional mystical and cosmological text describing the Tree of Life.

## The Voices from the Void
Lines from the *Sepher Yetzirah* (ascribed to Rabbi Akibah, *circa* second century AD), assembled from various translations.

1 In Thirty-Two wondrous Paths of Wisdom did Yah, Yahveh Tzabaoth (Lord of Hosts), the Gods of Israel, the Elohim (Living Ones), the King of Ages, the merciful and gracious God, the Exalted One, the Dweller in Eternity, most high and holy, engrave his Name by the Three Sepharim [harmonics of manifestation] – Numbers, Letters, and Sounds.

2 Ten are the (ineffable Sephiroth or Spheres) Voices from the Void.

Twenty-two are the Letters, the Foundation of all things; there are Three Mothers, Seven Double, and Twelve Simple Letters.

3  The Voices from the Void are Ten, so are the numbers; and as there are in man five fingers upon five, so over them is established a covenant of strength, by word of mouth, and by circumcision.

4  Ten is the number of the Voices from the Void, Ten and not nine, Ten and not eleven. Understand this wisdom, and be wise in its perception. Search out concerning it, restore the Word to the Creator, and replace him who formed it upon his throne.

5  The Ten Voices from the Void have Ten vast regions bonded to them; boundless in origin and without end; an abyss of good and evil, measureless height and depth; unbounded to the East and to the West; unbounded to the North and to the South; and the Lord, the one God, the Faithful King, rules all these from his holy Throne for ever and ever.

6  The Ten Voices from the Void appear as a flash of lightning; their origin is unseen and without end. The Word is in them as they emanate and return, they speak as from the whirlwind and on returning fall prostrate in adoration before the Throne.

7  The Ten Voices from the Void, whose end is in their beginning, arise like fire from burning coal. For God is superlative in unity, there is no equal to Him; what number may be placed before One?.

8  Ten are the Voices from the Void; let your lips be sealed lest you speak of them, let your heart be guarded as you meditate upon them; if your mind runs away bring it back under your control; even as it is said, running and returning, as the living creatures, and so is the Covenant made.

9  The Voices from the Void give out Ten numbers. First the Spirit of the Gods of the Living; blessed and more than blessed be the Living God of Ages. The Voice, the Spirit, the Word, these are of the Holy Spirit.

Second from the Spirit He produced Air, and within it shaped Twenty-Two sounds ... the letters. Three are Mothers, Seven are Double, and Twelve are Simple, but the Spirit is first above all these.

Third from the Air He shaped the Waters, and from the formless void shaped mud and clay, designed surfaces upon them, and hewed out hollows within them, so forming the powerful material Foundation.

Fourth from the Water he shaped Fire, and made a Throne of Glory with Auphanim (Wheels), Seraphim (Flaming Serpents), and Chioth Ha Qadesh (Holy Living Creatures), as his ministers. And with these three He completed His dwelling, so it is written: 'Who makes his angels spirits and his ministers a flaming fire'.

He chose Three from among the simple letters and sealed them, forming them into the great Name of IHV, and with this he sealed the universe in the six directions.

Fifth: He looked above and sealed the Height with IHV.

Sixth: He looked below and sealed the Depth with IVH.

Seventh: He looked before him and sealed the East with HIV.

Eighth: He looked behind and sealed the West with HVI.

Ninth: He looked to the right and sealed the South with VIH.

Tenth: He looked to the left and sealed the North with VHI.

10   Behold, from the Ten Ineffable Sephiroth proceed the One Spirit of the Gods of living Air, Water, Fire, and Height, Depth, East, West, North, and South.

## A Brief Commentary on the Verses

1   The universal Being is defined, or we should say more accurately defines itself, by various names, which in themselves are states, stages, and divine entities; the titles are not mere praises or idle honorifics, but precise definitions and aspects of divinity. Perhaps the most obvious detail for the modern reader is that divinity is plural: from a single Being multiple divinities emanate.

Three harmonics or cycles of manifestation are technically defined in the ancient text: *Numbers, Letters, Sounds*. We find the use of number, letter (*shape with inherent power and meaning*), and sound in many variants of creation mythology. Another typical example is Plato's *Myth of Er* (Appendix 3), which shares several concepts with the *Sepher Yetzirah*.

The *Sepher Yetzirah* is extremely precise in its application and combination of numbers, letters, and sounds, for they are rooted in an ancient Kabbalistic tradition of instruction and enlightenment. The *Thirty-two Paths* referred to are the ten stages (Spheres) and twenty-two links or combinations (Paths) of universal energy found upon the Tree of Life (see Figure 5). Thus we have originative divinity engraving its identity, Name, through three modes (numbers, letters, sounds) to define thirty-two Paths of Wisdom. The Paths represent the totality of the created and manifested universe, so the first verse takes us through the entire creation from Origination to Manifestation. The verses which follow elaborate upon each stage of the process.

2 The Ten Spheres of the Tree of Life, or *Sephiroth*, also translatable as *Ten Voices* or utterances from the void or chaos, are the major stages of universal manifestation, from the Void itself, through to the material substance. The Twenty Letters (of the Hebrew sacred alphabet) are allocated to the Paths or connections between each Sphere. If we use the analogy of utterance or voices for the Spheres, the Paths are the *interactive resonance* between them; once again this theory is defined by Plato, possibly drawing upon a Pythagorean creation myth (see page 168). Although the system of the *Sepher Yetzirah* is more complex than that of Plato, they are clearly related to one another upon a fundamental level.

3 The number Ten is reaffirmed, and is shown to relate to the creation of the human body, which is a mirror or harmonic of the universal body.

4 The mystical power of the Ten Spheres or Utterances is affirmed as a route towards enlightenment and universal perfection.

5 The text now proceeds with the allocation of metaphysical Directions: a typical theme in creation mythology throughout the world. The Ten Voices or Utterances (Spheres shown on the Tree of Life) each have a *vast region* attuned or bonded to their resonance; these regions are defined but without physical boundary. The map is that of Above/ Below/ East/ West/ South/ North, giving the familiar Six Directions (see Figure 7).

Ten zones are defined in the verse as follows:

I       Boundless Origin
II      Unending (Time)
III     Good (positive power potential)
IV      Evil (negative power potential)
V       Measureless Height
VI      Measureless Depth
VII     East
VIII    West

IX   North
X    South

They are linked in pairs:

1. Boundless Origin/   Unending (Time)
2. Good/   Evil
3. Measureless Height/   Depth
4. East/   West
5. North/   South

These pairs or polarities of Being may be further interpreted as:

1. (Pre-Time) Time
2. Energy (events)
3. Space
4 and 5 further 'engrave' or define interactions (events) within space
   and time.

We may now return to verse 6. The Lightning Flash is the traditional
shape or symbol taught in mystical instruction: it flashes 'down' the
Tree of Life, in the order 1-2-3-4-5-6-7-8-9-10. This primal Tree of Life
pattern is found on the earliest illustrations, and the more complex Paths
and Abyss patterns are generally later developments. Philosophically and
mathematically, this tenfold utterance or energy pattern is related to
that of the Pythagorean *Tetractys*, in which ten points of unfolding
number or creation form a triangular pattern (one point at the crown,
then two equidistant below it, then three below the two, and four below
three, totalling ten). The Tetractys and the Tree of Life are variants of
one another.

The Voices, however, emanate and return without end: the linear
sequence is an illusory property of our limited human field of awareness.
The original Word, the first utterance of Being from Non-Being, is
inherent within the Voices. The imagery is that of a whirlwind or vortex
of utterances or energies; in traditional terms they are also deities, the
multiple forms and names of God.

7   This verse again affirms the ultimate Unity of Being. It also refers
to certain mystical techniques of arousing energy within the human
organism, which are said to be a reflection of the universal forces of
creation. The Elemental codes and training programme in Chapter 14
are one expression of such techniques.

8 The instructional and devotional tone of verse 7 is given a definite form in verse 8: this refers to a specific meditational technique in which the human consciousness is brought into resonance with the primal Being or universal consciousness

9 The text now proceeds to enumerate and define the further stages of Creation, progressing to those of Number. The first Number, One, is that of the Living Spirit.

10 The second Number, Two, derives from One, and is the spiritual element of Air. Within this spiritual air are shaped the twenty letters (Paths), which are allocated to those of the Hebrew alphabet. Thus language and writing are in themselves sacred and magical, for they constantly reiterate or re-create the universe.

Third, from Air, the Waters are shaped. (These are the stages of Creation referred to in the Book of Genesis in the Christian Old Testament, drawing upon Hebrew ancient sources.) Within this third phase, the material Foundation is shaped, which will become the manifested worlds of matter.

Fourth, from Water, Fire is shaped. The Wheels, Flaming Serpents, and Holy Living Creatures are angelic entities, referred to in the Vision of Ezekiel and other mystical texts. These entities of pure force define and delimit and enable all energies within the Foundation of form. This phase of creation, therefore, mirrors the polarized patterns stated in the earlier verses, but always in more specific forms.

The next stage of creation describes the allocation of rotations or cycles of the divine Name to the Four Directions. This *sealing* creates an abstract cube with six faces, within the universal unlimited sphere of Being.

The divine force, however, is not traditionally regarded as 'abstract' but as a living presence: in Kabbalistic mysticism each rotation of a divine name causes different combinations of energy to arise and resonate.

# 10 Music, Tarot, the Axis Mundi

The foundations of tarot are, on first analysis, twofold, though the two branches arise out of one root and are not in any way antagonistic or separate. The first pattern inherent in tarot is physical, psychological, but most of all, cosmological: it reveals the ancient cycle of the Four Elements, which is found to rotate around the central pivot of the Axis Mundi, the spindle of the Worlds. This essentially mathematical expression generates the numbers 1 to 10 in the number cards of tarot, while the four suites of Swords, Rods, Cups, and Shields, or their variants in different decks of cards, represent expressions of the Four Elements of Air, Fire, Water, and Earth.

The spindle or Axis Mundi, around which these spiralling numbers form infinite combinations and patterns, is expressed by three of the Major Cards, or Trumps. These are The Moon, The Sun, and The Star. Despite the obvious presence of the Axis Mundi in both Renaissance, medieval, and classical cosmology, relatively modern expositions of tarot have persisted in the most bizarre and antagonistic relationships between tarot cards, particularly upon the Tree of Life, which is nothing more nor less than the Kabbalistic representation of the Axis Mundi or World Tree.

Even if we dispose of all varying systems found in collected literature, we can establish the concept of the Axis Mundi by simple common sense directly from the relationship between humanity, the microcosm, and the universe, the macrocosm. A human standing upon the surface of the planet Earth perceives three worlds or phases of relationship: that identified with the Moon, that identified with the Sun, and that identified with Stars, or with specific stellar locations. This is not ethereal metaphysics, but crude physical observation: from the Earth, to the Moon, Sun, Stars. The crudity of the observation is deceptive, however, for it is inseparable from properties of consciousness and inner states or conditions of heightened perception.

The upright position, the standing human echoing the alignment of

Moon, Sun, and Star at certain key times in the cycle of the solar system, is further defined by a sphere of real and multi-dimensional directions: East, South, West, and North. Three levels or spirals of this sphere are known, represented by three further trumps, the *Three Wheels* of Fortune, Justice, and Judgement. These are harmonics of one another, a truth reflected in the general language, the words we use for the cards and their concepts. They are also represented by three Goddesses in the ancient pantheons.

Within this basic pattern there is much that is musical, harmonic, relational, and practical.

## Music and Tarot

How does the empowerment of music relate to that ubiquitous set of images and patterns, the tarot? Is there anything inherent within tarot that can help us to a deeper practical realization of music for inner transformation? It has long been customary to allocate musical notes to certain symbols, planets, and, in some meditational or magical systems, to tarot images. What exactly, if anything, does this imply? What is the origin of this tradition of allocating musical notes to tarot?

To come to an adequate realization of answers to such questions, we must first abandon most of the material currently in publication concerning tarot. Such material derives almost entirely, either at first hand or at various removes, from nineteenth-century publications or privately circulated (but later published) material by French and British occultists, and takes no account of many older sources directly or indirectly relating to tarot. Such older sources date from the Renaissance, in the form of the first historical tarot images on cards, and from much earlier traditions, in the form of similar images with similar functions and relationships to one another preserved in epic poems, tales, and songs.

It is upon this second and earlier level that we shall discover and restate promising material for inner work in meditation and visualization with music, and find that it connects quite naturally to the revival of classical arts, cosmology, and metaphysics occurring during the Renaissance, which gave rise to the painting of the first known tarot cards. It must be emphasized that the (tarot) images themselves, and the Elemental system which acts as a foundation for both tarot and the perennial concept of the Music of the Spheres, were in existence and wide circulation long before any actual cards may be dated.[12]

In an earlier chapter, we employed a model, an image, of an ancient temple, and considered what musical arts and disciplines might have been used there. Such a working model is not wild supposition, but based upon texts and traditions handed down from the ancient world in various forms, some of which are preserved even today. A key phrase that might be applied to all empowered music is *pattern-making*. Musical patterns, sonic symbols, were generated to harmonize certain individual, collective, natural, and planetary forces. This tradition survives in a very attenuated form even in orthodox Christianity, where church music is employed to 'praise God', or to harmonize with universal Being.

On a more subtle level religious music should inspire the congregation, and raise their consciousness, even if only for a moment, to a rate that is not usually accessible in daily, habitual life.

Both the raising of rates of consciousness and the act of praising or harmonizing with greater Being were developed to a very powerful degree in ancient temple music and within spiritual and magical traditions involving music worldwide. The foundation of such artistic disciplines lay in using patterns of music which resonated in harmony with related patterns throughout nature, and ultimately came into harmony with universal patterns. There are a number of ways of initially approaching this art, though in developed work all such ways fuse together. Let us consider some of the principles involved.

## Inspirational Religious and Magical Music

Primal music is often inspirational: a sound is generated or uttered according to energies arising within or flowing through the individual or group. Such music is heard in the unconsidered or innocent utterances of the man or woman at work, though this type of daily music (as opposed to folk entertainment or specific story-telling songs) is virtually extinct in the West. Many of the most famous early sources recognizing this type of inspired utterance are in the writings of the early Christian Church, quoted and analysed in *Folksong Plainsong* by Father G. B. Chambers.[13]

We do have, however, examples of inspired or innocent musical utterance today in inspirational chanting and instrumental music among primal people, and (much rarer than we are led to believe) among certain religious sects. Caution should be exercised when listening to so-called inspirational, 'channelled' or charismatic music on record, as it is frequently contrived.

More relevant is the unavoidable fact that true inspirational music is a matter of *being there*; many of the energies inherent in the inspirational event are subtle and cannot be pressed into vinyl. We have, therefore, a situation in which an energy inspires and causes a musical event, through the medium of the human organism and consciousness. The earliest religious music was not, of course, 'religious' in the modern sense; it consisted of utterances or truths in musical patterns, the voice of humanity in harmony with the voice of Nature, and therefore in an octave relationship to the voice of universal Being.

Primal inspirations, however, are not always sufficient in themselves for deep empowerment or transformation through music. Furthermore, they may not affect third parties, as is the intention in highly energized magical, spiritual, or meditative music, which is consciously intended to have a specific, deeply transformative effect upon other people, or upon the environment beyond the immediate individual or group uttering or generating the music. More important than this, however, is the unavoidable truth that inspiration does not always come, and that the best of primal patterns may and do become warped out of their pristine or original shape. It is at this stage that a disciplined spiritual or magical music becomes important, to reattune us to the primal sound within.

Pure inspirational utterances are the simplest foundation for the use of musical tones in contemplation: a certain pitch or musical pattern attunes to and resonates within a certain corresponding state of consciousness. In ancient tradition, much time and effort was spent in exploring the inner dimensions, the metaphysical worlds, both through meditation, visualization, ritual, and other means such as inner-world contact. The patterns found in such explorations were expressed as musical keys, always in tune with deepest intuition concerning the music of the solar system itself. This inherent music is heard with the whole being, not merely with the ears. It is the origin of the much-discussed Music of the Spheres, which is the inherent music of the Solar System, leading to harmonic interaction with the stars beyond.

## Music and Images

A large proportion of inner tradition and magical or spiritual discipline requires and employs specific, highly developed sets of images. The human imagination, our ability to generate pictures within our consciousness, is a very potent force indeed, and we are only beginning to reassess it today after several centuries in which the power of the imagination was set aside as being trivial or even degenerate. If music has the potential to be inspired within us by certain forces, concepts of Being, or through contact with higher entities, then our imagination provides images, pictures, that attune and correspond to these pure forces. So potent images are often closely linked with sound.

If we consider the arts of visualization in world religion, we find a regular and intentional fusion of images and sounds. Certain hymns, chants, liturgical musics, are intentionally related to specific images of gods, goddesses, inner landscapes, events, stories. We also find this fusion upon a more humble level in oral tradition; the great epic tales and ballads, which in themselves often preserve early mythic sequences and the material of older religions, are always chanted or sung. Somewhere within this fusion lies the key to using tarot and music for the present day.

If we are to use music for inner growth and transformation, we should develop our empowering techniques and abilities in harmony with our imagination; the two forces are not inseparable, but generally work very closely together. Furthermore, there is a curious property inherent in both imagination and memory, for if these faculties are intentionally aligned to certain sets of images, then they will eventually regenerate such images in new patterns in a powerful manner.[14]

Tarot images mirror specific forces within the human entity, the interaction of spirit and soul, psyche and body. The use of tarot for trivial fortune-telling is its lowest possible level of application, and should be ignored by anyone wishing to find the deeper, more powerful uses of tarot and the imagination. If we link sets of images, such as pantheons, Elemental cycles, tarot, religious emblems, and so forth to musical patterns, we can generate a very powerful interaction within ourselves, either individually or in group work.

Tarot incorporates an Elemental cycle, which is, of course, the basis of music, and a planetary cycle, which is inherent in music in a solar context, the tradition of hearing and reiterating the Music of the Spheres. Out of such tarot cycles or reiterated patterns, directly analogous to those of music, arise images. The images in tarot are of mythic entities, gods and goddesses, or, in a Jungian sense, of archetypes, potent representations of forces that are generally unconscious.

In our present context, however, the word archetype should really be used in its original, proper, and precise sense, in which it refers to the matrices or universal moulding and shaping patterns inherent within Creation, within the universe examined both by physics and metaphysics. Traditionally archetypes (in the true sense of the word) are represented by the Elemental system, and by sacred geometry or metaphysical topology. Such mapping techniques are inherent within perennial, anonymous systems such as tarot, the Tree of Life, and the Platonic solids; today we find them 'discovered', through their undeniable existence in nature, by modern physics, genetics, holography,

Figure 6

# The Axis Mundi and Tarot Images

TRUMP RELATIONSHIPS: The Cycle of Ascent and Descent

*Partners or polar pairs of Trumps*

| A | 14 | Hermit – Innocent | 15 | D |
|---|---|---|---|---|
| S | 13 | Hanged Man – Temperance | 16 | E |
| C | 12 | Death – Emperor | 17 | S |
| E | 11 | Tower – Strength | 18 | C |
| N | 10 | Guardian – Empress | 19 | E |
| D | 9 | Chariot – Lovers | 20 | N |
| I | 8 | Magician – Priestess | 21 | D |
| N | 7 | Fool – Universe | 22 | I |
| G | | | | N |
| | | | | G |

*Ultimate or extreme pairs of Trumps*

| 7 | Fool – Innocent | 15 |
|---|---|---|
| 8 | Magician – Temperance | 16 |
| 9 | Chariot – Emperor | 17 |
| 10 | Guardian – Strength | 18 |
| 11 | Tower – Empress | 19 |
| 12 | Death – Lovers | 20 |
| 13 | Hanged Man – Priestess | 21 |
| 14 | Hermit – Universe | 22 |

## BASIC TABLE OF TRUMPS

*Three Worlds*
1  Moon
2  Sun
3  Star

*Three Wheels*
4  Fortune
5  Justice
6  Judgement

*Ascending or
Internalizing Trumps*
7  Fool
8  Magician
9  Chariot
10  Guardian
11  Tower
12  Death
13  Hanged Man
14  Hermit

*Descending or
Externalizing Trumps*
15  Innocent
16  Temperance
17  Emperor
18  Strength
19  Empress
20  Lovers
21  Priestess
22  Universe

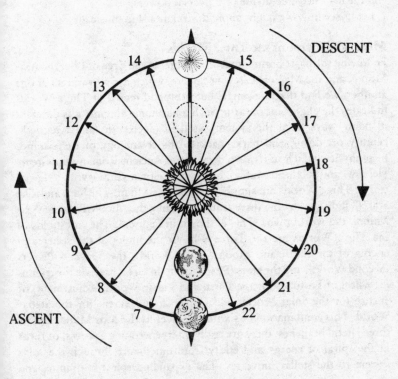

and other branches of mathematics and science that reveal new insights, coming full circle into various harmonically related restatements of ancient world-models or cosmologies and cosmogonies.[15]

The images which rise out of these archetypical patterns and inter-actions of energy are not archetypes in themselves, but *eidolons* or *telesmata*, the forms by which gods and goddesses, for example, present themselves within the human imagination.

This is not such a difficult concept, for it is simply one of personae or masks, or working forms. By way of comparison we need only to remind ourselves that no human being, after all, appears exactly as he or she is, and the body form is only temporary and transitory. Such a variety and fluidity of outer form reflects an inner reality. Tarot images, therefore, embody or give form (usually but not exclusively anthro-pomorphic) within the human imagination. What they give form to are archetypical forces or energies of the universe, which have, in themselves, a mirror within the human entity. Tarot images and other telesmata, therefore, act as interfaces between the microcosmic human energies, and the macrocosmic divine or universal powers.

Let us see how we might apply this relationship musically.

## Music and Tarot in the Three Worlds

Following the basic harmonic relationships of the Tree of Life, the Axis Mundi, and the Magical Circle or Sphere, which are all variants of one another, we find that the simple but profound model of Three Worlds indicates the alignment of tarot. Such a harmonic alignment is different in many ways from the systems used in nineteenth- and twentieth-century occultism, and harks back to the cosmology of Renaissance metaphysics, which in its turn drew upon Ancient Roman and Greek, Hebrew, and folkloric sources, including Celtic mythology.

The Three Worlds are simply those of The Moon, The Sun, and The Star(s), indicated by the three trumps forming the Middle Pillar or Axis Mundi, the world pivot. This is shown in Figure 6. The thresholds of the Three Worlds are the Three Wheels, the limits of the spheres of energy of the Earth and Moon (Third World), the Sun and Planets (Second World), and the Stars (First World). In tarot these are the trumps of Wheel of Fortune, for the Earth and Lunar World, Adjustment, or Justice for the Solar World, and Universal Judgement for the Stellar World. This combination of six images gives us the Axis Mundi and its three lateral branches: these are really interpenetrating Spheres, or turns of the spiral of energy and entity from our planet through the solar system to the stellar universes. The expanding spiral is infinite, and works upon a cycle of octaves, with other proportions within each spiral of octaves.

In the system of Elemental Tones and Chants described in Chapter 14 we find that each of the Three Worlds has a mode, an octave of notes in a specific relationship. By running through the entire cycle of modes we reach from the Earth to the stellar universe. As we have seen, six universal images are allocated as the trumps of Moon, Sun, Star, Fortune, Justice, Judgement. These are resonated as modes, with one Element as the primary energy upon each level. The levels are centred upon the planets or spheres of Earth, Moon, Sun, and Crown (Star), with the primary Elemental natures of Earth, Water, Fire, and Air, as follows:

4.  Earth/ Earth
3.  Moon/ Water
2.  Sun/ Fire
1.  Star/ Air

The Earth Mode is, for practical purposes, identical to a scale of C major. The Lunar Mode is the mode of D–D, commencing one tone above Earth, with no adjustment (i.e. playable all on keyboard white notes). The Solar Mode runs from E–E, and the Steller Mode from F–F. For further details of this sequence see Chapter 14.

If we examine the Tree of Life, we find that it consists of three zones, with spheres connecting to central hubs, like the spokes of a wheel. The centres are primarily that of The Moon (Third Triad), The Sun (Second Triad), and The Crown or First Star (First Triad). These connective or harmonic relationships are traditionally called the Paths, and it is to these that tarot trumps have frequently been allocated.

As we have seen, the paths between Earth and Moon (tenth and ninth Spheres), and Moon and Sun (ninth and sixth Spheres), and Sun and Crown (sixth and first Spheres) are clearly the trumps of Moon, Sun, and Star, the pivot of the cosmos, the Axis Mundi. Their thresholds are the Three Wheels of Fortune (between Mercury and Venus, or the eighth and seventh Spheres), Justice (between Mars and Jupiter, Severity and Mercy, or the fifth and fourth Spheres), and Judgement (between Understanding and Wisdom, Saturn and the Zodiac, the third and second Spheres).

As there are 22 trumps, this leaves a further 16 images for the remaining 16 Paths. In the present system of harmonic relationship between the Trumps and Paths, we concentrate upon polarity, and octave and proportional relationships between the images. This has already been shown in the six universal trumps described, and is revealed within the remaining trumps as follows:

Fool/ Universe 8–10–7
Magician/ Priestess 8–9–7
Chariot/ Lovers 8–6–7
Tower/ Strength 5–6–4
Hanged Man/ Temperance 3–6–2

These triadic polarized relationships, generally defined by the imagery and the sexual polarity of the pairs of trumps, are joined by the Right- and Left-hand Pillar Trumps. The Right-hand trumps are anabolic or building energies, while the Left-hand trumps are catabolic or destroying (purifying) energies. Once again, the sequence harmonizes three spirals, rising from the Earth to the Stellar octaves.

Fool/ Universe 8–10–7 (as above)
Guardian (Pan or Devil) 8–5/ Empress (Flower Maiden) 7–4
Death (originally Female) 5–3/ Emperor (Life King) 4–2
Hermit 3–1/ Hierophant (originally Female, Sophia or Inno-
   cent) 2–1

To pursue this harmonic structure of tarot further, the reader should lay the trumps out in the patterns described. Further details of these harmonic relationships are found in my book and deck (illustrated by Miranda Gray) *The Merlin Tarot*.[12]

To work with musical empowerment and tarot is a most powerful and rewarding technique, though it takes some patience and discipline to grasp the wide range of images and combinations involved. It may be broadly divided into work with Aces and Number Cards, and Trumps and Court Cards, though in advanced work various fusions of sets of cards may be used.

This method of imaginative and Elemental work has little or no connection with superficial fortune-telling, and uses tarot images upon a more potent level of energy and consciousness. If you are used to using tarot for generalized fortune-telling, then this method may take a little longer to establish, as it cuts through those widely popularized levels of symbolism and interpretation normally used in predictive systems.

## Aces and Number Cards

These are the basic numbers of the Four Elements, from 1 to 10, through their fourfold cycle. Taking any satisfactory tarot deck, the basic rotations and numbers correspond to the spiral of notes as shown in Figure 2. The meditator lays out cards and meditates upon their qualities while uttering the relevant pitched tone and vowel sound.

For raw Elemental power, the Four Aces, which usually represent Implements of balance and control (Sword or Arrow for Air/ Rod or Wand for Fire/ Cup for Water/ Shield or Mirror for Earth), are used with the root Elemental calls in the Planetary modes (see Figure 1).

## Trumps and Court Cards

### Trumps

The trumps are laid out according to the Axis Mundi and Three Worlds. The meditator or visualizer then chooses one or more trumps for work; if more than one is chosen they should reveal a harmonic or polarized relationship.

The image or images are then built strongly in visualization while uttering the appropriate Elemental calls in the mode of the relevant World (i.e. Lunar, Solar, Stellar). Any trump will resonate to one, two, three, or all four Elements. Some very fine tuning of inner energies and imaginative forces is possible through work with this technique, for the subtle effect of each trump alters according to the Element or Elements aroused through chant.

The inherent significance of each trump is greatly enhanced by using the Three Worlds cosmology and psychology, and the student may find it valuable to work with intuitive interpretations based upon actual card pictures and their attributes and the harmonic relationships described above, rather than plough through the vast range of contradictory tarot literature for 'meanings'.

### Court Cards

The court cards represent both archetypes and human personality types. In meditation and visualization we must first decide which level we will use them on. Each card relates to the Elements, and represents an Elemental archetype or personality mode, usually as follows: King = Fire/ Queen = Water/ Knight = Air/ Page = Earth. Each suite is of an Element in itself, thus a King of Fire is Fire of Fire, a Page of Earth is Earth of Earth, and so forth. Once again, Elemental tones and calls may be used along with visualization or meditation based upon the images. Before working with any of the foregoing techniques and combinations of tarot images, the reader or student should spend some time with basic Elemental call and chant training, as set out in Chapter 14.

# 11    Crystals, Time, Stars

The use of crystals as media for energy is central to our era. In technology we have seen the use of quartz crystals revolutionize computing and automation. These pages have been written on a computer, written using quartz crystal technology. The use of large computers to make fractal calculations or predict weather patterns has led to a series of 'revelations' concerning apparently chaotic or so-called random patterns and their mathematics, revelations which are merely computerized proofs of the ancient traditional teaching of holisms, universal patterns. Such patterns reflect and reiterate themselves no matter how far apart we attempt to dissect or how violently we try to destroy. Thus the advent of the computer, a device which has been regarded with gravest suspicion by many spiritual teachers as it seems to replace human awareness with a machine, has paradoxically enabled proof, in the materialist sense, of holistic patterns within universal mathematics and physics. All this through agitating crystals, causing them to vibrate at known speeds and so drive computing devices.

In music we have seen this new technology make remarkable changes, for computers and music seem, in some ways, to be ideally suited to one another. We shall return to the complex question of synthesizers in Appendix 2, but it is worth considering briefly that computerized music is operated through the vibration of quartz crystals, and that certain categories of technical achievement, or at least potential achievement, undreamed of by previous generations of musicians and composers, are now possible with a relatively simple personal computer.

While this microtechnological revolution has been flourishing, another rapidly expanding utilization of crystals has also taken place. There has been a widely publicized and heavily commercialized upsurge in the use of crystals for what might be loosely termed esoteric purposes. Crystals are now widely employed in many types of alternative therapy; they are found in meditative or visualizing practices; and literature on the techniques and categories of crystal-working abound. Such literature ranges from reasonably intelligent and practical to absurdly puerile and whimsical.

If we pause to examine the wide range of books, booklets, kits, and shop goods relating to crystals, we find that most, though we might stress not all, of this crystalline revolution exists in a New Age vacuum. It is not rooted into deep spiritual or magical traditions, but is primarily a matter of fashion, of enthusiasms, and of commercialism.

It seems odd that while we have a very materialist, precise, and well-researched and developed use of crystals in technology, we also have an almost entirely ephemeral and non-analytical use of crystals in fashionable esoteric techniques. These two branches of crystal knowledge do not seem to refer very often to one another, though the new developments in mathematical patterns such as fractal images, strange-attractors, and similar computable holisms, visibly presented from what was for long assumed to be 'chaos', represent a major fusion of esoteric tradition and materialist calculation. More simply, they prove, in a materialist sense (for they are shown upon a monitor screen therefore they *must* be true!), concepts which have been taught for thousands of years in the world's magical and spiritual disciplines.

The current surge of frivolity concerning crystals masks a number of serious uses in magical and psychic fields which have been taught and developed since the earliest times. Regrettably, modern crystal theorists and practitioners seem totally unaware of these existing teachings, other than in the highly commercialized context of crystal sciences in Ancient Atlantis.

On a personal note, I was taught a typical operative tradition involving crystals in the 1960s, of the kind known to magical or psychic disciplines worldwide; no one at that time realized that crystal-working would explode into such a trivialized and, dare we say it, lucrative market.

The teaching which I received at that time was merely part of a large holistic tradition of magical theory and practice, in which crystal-working, possible Atlantean history or visions, and Elemental music were taken almost for granted, simply tools to learn and use in the endless task of inner transformation. There was no shrill declaration of revelation or potential New Age-ness; these were arts and disciplines that had been in existence, in various expressions, for millennia, with their constituents taught orally, through meditation and vision, and scattered through many sources in early literature, poetry, tales, music, and song. The precise techniques and their inner keys are always part of whatever close or hidden tradition the student enters into, but a general core tradition is found worldwide.

Upon entering a New Age such techniques move into a higher octave, a further spiral, serving the same ends, which are those of spiritual realization, but in a higher or more potent form. They are not in themselves part of a new revelation, but are simply tools or enabling methods that come to the foreground of collective awareness in certain time periods or cultures, and recede in others.

## Crystals are Music

There are a number of methods found in esoteric tradition concerning crystals, colours, musical tones, and patterns. As a rule these are related to the septenary or sevenfold system, which corresponds to the seven planets, the seven locations (i.e. the six directions of East/ South/ West/ North/ Above/ Below, and the seventh metaphysical locus within). Seven colours or rays are said to attune to seven levels of energy within the human entity; these in turn correspond to zones within the aura, psychic centres, power foci on the Tree of Life or Axis Mundi, and segments of the Elemental Sphere and Circle. They are frequently given correspondences to the seven basic steps of a musical scale or mode, though such a correspondence is better employed in the context of modes than of a fixed, rigid, Westernized and quite modern type of scale. (See Chapter 14 for a full set of modes and Elemental patterns which may be used in chanting or instrumental music for changing consciousness. For historic reference purposes a number of tables and theories by authors in previous centuries, or taught within relatively anonymous magical traditions, are found in Joscelyn Godwin's *Music, Magic and Mysticism*[16] and my own *Music and the Elemental Psyche*.[1])

Variations occur, as we would expect, within differing systems or tables of correspondence, but the fundamental structures and concepts plainly have a unity and persistence that should not be passed over or trivialized. They derive from enduring deep intuitions and research into the holism of consciousness and energy within the environment, be it the environment of the body, the land, the planet, the solar system or the universe. Like the reiterating patterns discovered by new mathematics and demonstrated upon the computer screen, one part is harmonically and paradoxically identical to the whole; no matter how relatively large or small we think to divide such entities, their wholeness, even when beyond our perception and accessible only through logarithms and visual analogies, remains.

Before presenting some of the esoteric teachings concerning crystals, we should explore the knowledge available at the threshold (or perhaps nowadays we should call it fusion-zone) of esoteric arts and disciplines and materialist science. Paradoxically we find this most modern of fusions by reaching into the distant past, for we begin in the megalithic era.

## Standing Stones and Crystals

We do not know what type of music was uttered or played by the megalithic peoples who built their vast civilization across Western Europe. It has been customary for historians and hard-line archaeologists to suggest that they were brutish, primitive people; we might therefore assume that they had little or no musical perception or creation. The hard-line attitude, which is really nothing more nor less than the juvenile product of propaganda, is now beginning to evaporate. The building of the megalithic structures was a technical achievement that could hardly be equalled today, taking a social organization spanning many lifetimes and implying knowledge that directly contradicts our erroneous image of ignorant savages or primitive people.

There are a number of esoteric and simple factual concepts concerned with megalithic sacred sites that relate directly to music and metaphysics, and which may be developed in modern use. First, we find that many sites were aligned to specific stars and planets, a tradition that was perpetuated in later ages by the alignment of classical temples in Ancient Greece and Rome, and indeed in the building of the great religious buildings of Christianity, particularly the Gothic abbeys. Enough has been said about the Music of the Spheres and the harmonic orbits of the planets as proportions of the holism, the entire choir of the solar system, to suggest that this alignment has many implications.

When we consider the subject of crystals, there are many significant finds, archaeologically, connected to ancient cultures. The most dramatic are the mysterious crystal skulls from ancient South American civilizations, perhaps deriving from Atlantean culture. But there is a much wider and more significant use of millions of crystals within the megalithic cultures, still widely visible, and applicable, today. Anyone visiting a megalithic site can test this for themselves, and it has implications for modern work using crystals that can be developed in private. The most common stone used in many of the ancient megalithic sacred sites or temples was a type of granite containing quartz crystals: a single standing stone of such a granite crystalline rock contains a very large number of tiny crystals.

This frequent choice of crystalline rock might be mere coincidence, of course, but the enduring traditions and beliefs concerning crystals, and the modern rediscovery or technical applications of quartz, imply otherwise. In any case, we can make a few simple factual assertions concerning stone structures with a high crystalline content, such as ancient standing stones and stone circles. When we combine these simple facts with musical harmonic implications, and then with the alignment of many such sites with planetary and stellar patterns, a powerful musical potency or resonance is suggested.

## The Natural Music of Crystals

The proportions inherent within crystals are essentially the same as those of music. This is a simple mathematical matter, though in our present context we are not concerned with discussion or examples of actual formulae but with the simple fact of such proportional relationships. The angles and the proportions between the sides and planes of crystals reveal those known through music. There are a number of textbooks discussing this proportionality, and the theory is by no means a recent one.[17]

Indeed, the inherent musicality of crystals was known to the Renaissance alchemists, for as recent research has shown, the alchemical varnish used on the violins made by Stradivarius had finely powdered crystals as a component. Modern instruments now being made, and using a similar varnish with powdered crystal, produce that remarkable tone quality which was, until recently, assumed to be uniquely that of Stadivarius. Rumour has it that the inflated market value of the old violins has been shaken by this discovery.

Why does the presence of crystals in a varnish enhance the tone qualities of an instrument? What connection does this have to alchemy, and to the standing stones of the megalithic culture, dating from at least as early as 3,000 BC? To answer these questions we must consider some of the simplest basics of crystalline structure.

We can begin with the simple assertion of the oscillation of atoms: atoms are harmonic oscillators. In a musical model of the atom, which is exactly that defined by modern physics (though obviously we are using very general, non-technical definitions here), the nuclei could be said to oscillate. The orbits of the electrons reverberate to the periodic harmonic motions of the nuclei. This harmonic law of proportion and reverberation was that employed by Johannes Kepler, using musical measurement to establish the orbits of the planets. It works as a proportional model on an atomic scale, and on a planetary or solar scale.

These proportions, sets of relationships in motion, are inherent in music. They are found in the expanding spiral of octaves (see Figure 2), just as they are found in the spiral of a nebula.

In crystals the molecular lattice is highly defined, giving the precise and much-discussed properties of shape and energy within any crystalline growth. This in itself gives rise to music, though of a limited nature. The molecules of crystals may move only along certain axes, and such movement or agitation causes a further movement in the surrounding air. This is, by definition, music rather than noise, for the shape of a crystal and its proportional limits mean that its movement and the vibrations communicated to a surrounding medium (air) are strict and set within certain limits.

A crystal can be vibrated with a bow, such as a violin bow, or it can be set into motion with a hammer or other striking object. This artificial movement of the crystal will amplify its inherent musical definition, sometimes causing an audible sound. Other factors which we cannot technically approach here are the three crystalline axes, often described as electrical, mechanical, and optical. If the mechanical axis is changed through exterior energy being applied, the other axes may respond with proportionally related changes. This is the basis of crystal chips being used as timing devices in computer technology.

Now, all of this, in non-technical terminology, implies that if we utter a musical note or impel a crystal with an exterior force, we cause energetic changes to occur according to certain well-defined proportions. The crystal actually emits a constant musical vibration, and a constant electrical vibration, and also responds to and emits light. Usually the intensity of these vibrations is too minute to register upon the human senses, but it is present nevertheless.

In ancient alignments, made of crystalline rock, there will be millions and millions of such tiny 'voices'. They are physically located within masses of rock, aligned, in many cases, upon powerful foci of earth energy, such as springs, geomagnetic nodes, and other subtle power sources. Furthermore, they are aligned to stellar and planetary patterns. Thus we could say that the crystalline standing stones act as interfaces between the earth and the stars, and that their function is a musical one.

Although the modern revival of interest in the hidden powers of crystal tends towards very broad definition and so-called 'pure' crystals, it seems likely from all of the foregoing that the more complex a crystalline structure is, the more powerful it is, as a complex crystalline rock will have an infinite musical potential, while a highly polished and neatly hand-finished crystal will have a relatively limited musical potential.

This is a very important esoteric or metaphysical concept, inseparably linked to a physical and nowadays proven set of facts. Let us pursue it a little further, for we need consider only that in any stone or stone circle, or indeed in any building of later cultures employing a crystalline rock, there will be a vast number of tiny resonances, corresponding to the entire musical spectrum. This in itself may be unimportant, but when certain patterns or frequencies resonate through the structure as a whole, they will find a response in large numbers of the crystals. This is how the crystalline varnish enhances a stringed instrument.

Thus a stone complex is musically aligned upon several octaves of matter and energy. It has a very large number of crystalline resonances either in potential or in actual fact. These are upon certain geomagnetic nodes or harmonic sources of energy; the shape of the site itself and the alignments of the stones harmonize with certain stellar, planetary and solar events, cycles, and proportions. The factor that we might add now is the human one: if musical utterances are made at such sites, within a circle or directly into the stone themselves, they will cause a response in those crystals that can resonate in harmony or unison with the music uttered.

Just as the ancient megalithic sites were attuned to stellar and planetary frequencies, so we may use crystalline structures in our modern work with musical empowerment. The varnish used by Stradivarius enhanced the overtones of his instruments, due to the presence of the powdered crystal; the stones used by the ancients enhanced the subtle tones of the earth and stellar energies, due to the presence of millions of tiny crystals. The principle may be applied in individual work: if you seek to work with certain limited frequencies, use well-defined crystal with musical proportions that can be ascertained by experiment.

If you wish to work with variable frequencies, or to use crystal interfaces that change with the seasons, the stars, or your own work pattern, use clumps of crystals, or rough quartz rock. If such a rock comes from a sacred site or power centre, it will still resonate in tune with that location, even though you take it thousands of miles to another location. This size is irrelevant; quite small pieces from the ground will suffice. This is not an invitation to despoil sacred sites or geomagnetic power centres, but it is part of a well-established tradition that should be used with discretion and balance. If, for example, you know nothing about a site, it is not advisable to employ its crystalline rock.

Merely as an interesting aside, I can state that in the late 1960s I was taught to find a small fragment of natural crystalline rock, from a ridge close to where I lived at that time, on the edge of Exmoor in the south-west of England. I was told that traditionally magicians, seers or bards (call them what you will) selected such a small crystalline rock at the commencement of their training, and kept it for the rest of their lives. At a later stage it was used for direct tuition to pupils, playing back the energies, inner contacts, and patterns learned by the magician. The pupil in turn found a crystalline fragment for his or her training, which could be set into resonance with that of the teacher.

Traditionally, we are taught that the ancient stone sites hold within them the memories and magical and spiritual arts of the ancients, and may be used to tap into such knowledge. Nowadays, in the 1990s, this reiteration of energy by crystals is a proven and widely used fact of technology, albeit in limited manner.

# 12   Vowels, Breath, Energy

In ancient sacred texts the vowels were frequently omitted: in Jewish mystical and orthodox religious practices and texts, for example, great emphasis is placed upon the sacred quality of vowels.

In musical instruments the timbre of an instrument is defined by certain patterns of overtones in relationship to a fundamental (theoretical) note, a note that cannot independently exist without its overtones. Instrumental timbre, the tonal quality that defines the difference between instruments, is a vowel-like quality. Many emotional responses are achieved by the performer or composer through the use of certain instruments either as solo voices or in carefully studied combinations; particularly those that approach the timbre of the human voice with their vowel-like quality.

Vowels are the spirit of speech, of vocalizing, of pitched musical patterns made audible as sound in proportion. Without them we would have no speech (try speaking without a vowel! It simply cannot be done). The first exhalation of breath causes a vowel sound to be uttered. Junctions or thresholds thereafter are the consonants: vowels are open sounds, consonants are made by closing. In instrumental music, consonants, thresholds, are found in the attack of a wave-form, of a note, and in the articulation or musical punctuation of the performance. They are also, of course, provided by percussion, which in itself produces very complex tones, complex vowel sounds within the percussive rhythm.

To cut a long story short, we cannot utter speech or music without vowels, without open, resonating, harmonic sounds. We can and frequently do make such utterances with little or no use of consonants, though such a primal type of utterance becomes less prevalent as a culture increases in complexity. Magical calls and primal music tend towards elongated vowel sounds; the sounds of materialized society, and its music, tend towards consonants, closed and clustered barriers between shortened vowels. When the vowels are pitched, they become chant or, if given definite words, song. In instrumental music the vowel-like patterns can be very complex indeed, giving the colour or timbre of individual sounds.

The first impulse of the universe, uttering itself from the Void, is traditionally called the Breath (*Pneuma, Ruach Elohim*, the Holy Spirit). This First Breath, issuing outwards, uttered the first *opening* Sound, consisting of aspirants and vowels. In Kabbala this is sometimes defined as the Name AHIH, which is simply the sound of breathing, the Breath of Divine Being.

This metaphysical concept is more easily pursued in meditation than in verbal intellectualization, but let us explore it a little further, for it has many hidden potential insights. The originative impulse of the universe was traditionally understood to be Sound; therefore a universal utterance was described, in traditional mysticism and magic, in terms of the mechanism of sound production of the human voice. This seems quite practical as a tuitional model, particularly in cultures where mythic and poetic symbols, rather than mathematical formulae, were used to describe reality.

The tradition, however, is not merely one of analogy or metaphor; such concepts would have been incomprehensible or even abhorrent to the ancients. The human voice, and, indeed, any defined instrumental utterance, declares the operation of a universal Voice, through the law of octaves, through the reflection of the macrocosm within the microcosm. So we should dispose of any cosy notion of allegory, or arrogant assumptions that pre-science was grasping for words to express concepts which needed an as yet uninvented computer.

Modern physics has realized that the universe is emitted, uttered, set in motion, through a potency of simultaneous contraction and expansion. This potency, this unknown source of energy, space and time, utters the Sound, the Word, of ancient metaphysics. Thus when we utter a defined sound, or set a musical instrument in motion by applying energy to its components and so generating sound through air, we are echoing that First Breath and First Utterance.

Now, if we subscribe to the rationalist or materialist theory that there is a void, a spatial emptiness which is then filled (either with exploding stars, or in musical terms with sound), we become entrapped in all sorts of problems concerning the first explosion, the age, the amount of energy available and so forth.[15] The alternative picture is that of a *pleroma* as fullness in which expansion (positive) and contraction (negative) are simultaneous events, and within which *nodes* or energy patterns appear, interact, and demanifest. The fullness itself remains, to use an old term, transcendent yet immanent.

When we utter a sound, or cause a note to be emitted from an instrument, we create energy patterns, nodes, within the fullness. We do not cause a sound to rattle into emptiness, but rather take the existing fullness and shape it into a temporary (i.e. timed) pattern. This pattern works its way through certain combinations and reiterations, and eventually reverts to the fullness from which it was drawn. This conceptual model applies to music, to physical energies and entities, to human beings, to planets, to stars, to atoms. Certain proportions and typical nodal patterns are found through archetypes, orders or harmonic spirals of the universe. They imply to our understanding that they are overtones, undertones or partials of the primary nodal patterns of all Being, of the simultaneously creating and destroying fullness, and of the inclusive consciousness that it implies and that implies it.

None of these concepts is particularly abstruse or painful; they are merely at variance with the crippling linear conditioning that has 'educated' most Westerners, both in formal education and in daily life. Ironically, modern mathematics and physics seem to have proved (though not without endless and ongoing dispute over details) that the pleroma, the fullness, the simultaneity, is the true condition of the universe.

The human voice, therefore, by the law of octaves within the Fullness of Being, can and does utter the sounds of universal Being. This is really common sense (on one level), for whatever we do is part of *being*, our sound is part of Sound. The human will and imagination, however, act as mediating forces within the pleroma to cause certain shapes, certain sounds, to attune proportionally to the inherent utterance of the universe.

In traditional metaphysical or magical systems, an octave or proportional pattern was defined, by which we have earth, lunar, solar, and stellar scales or octaves. These are really nothing more or less than prime concepts that arise from standing upon the surface of our planet and looking into the universe. Note that we say 'into' and not 'up at'. Although up and down are used as locating concepts, due to the force of gravity, when we look towards the stars we are looking inwards, into the sphere of the universe. Albert Einstein established this concept of relativity for the modern intellect, though it has been stated in many different expressions through the ages and cannot, by its very nature, be a 'new discovery'.

Figure 7
# Breathing the Six Directions

Many of the most powerful esoteric or empowering arts are based upon deceptively simple concepts. The Six Directions are East, South, West, North, Above, and Below, with a seventh implied as Within. These are not, however, literal compass directions for accurate bearings: they are archetypical directions, relating to the position of a human being standing upon the surface of the planet. The relative position, defined by a sphere, is repeated at different octaves through the Three Worlds, Lunar, Solar, and Stellar. In this context they have a planetary and cosmological relevance: many creation myths and cosmological legends place a strong emphasis upon direction. The Six directions, therefore, are based upon the upright figure of a human being, with EAST: Before, SOUTH: Right, WEST: Behind, NORTH: Left. These archetypical directions correspond to the Four Quarters and Four Elements as shown in Figure 1.

The concept of Sacred Space and the Directions is inherent and explicitly built into ancient temples, aligned to stellar locations, and more recently abbeys and churches, usually aligned to the rising sun with the altar in the east. To use the concepts of Sacred Space and the Directions for meditation and visualization, as in the exercises described in Chapter 12, it is not essential to find accurate compass points. But a general alignment to the solar or Elemental directions, such as the rising sun at the East, is traditionally taught to be a highly effective way of working, as it aligns the human energies with those of the environment.

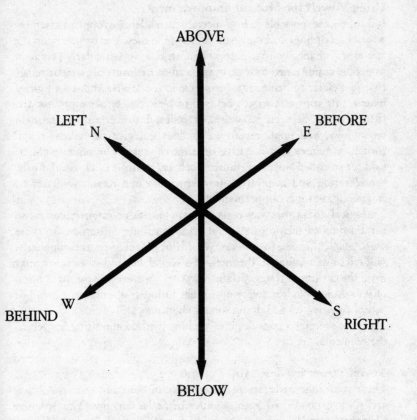

## Using Vowels for Musical Empowerment

It is, of course, possible to be a spectator, an idler. Anyone can assemble a list of recordings and suggest that plopping these one by one upon the stereo will change consciousness. This attitude is particularly prevalent in people conditioned to rock music and other forms of popular music that laid claim to being transformative in the 1960s. And, to a limited extent, this approach (much beloved of New Age books on music and therapy) can be seen to work. It relies, however, on a transient technology, and upon repetition. It does not give permanent transformation, either in a negative or positive sense. The same might be said for so-called 'superior' musics such as art music or classical music: the elevation and inspiration (or depression and nauseation) can be staggering, but it is not permanent.

Magical chant, by way of contrast, consists of uttering vowels in certain pitched relationships, and later of adding consonants to these sacro-magical tones, to generate Words of Power. Any anthropologist will tell us as much, and the method is well defined in esoteric writings from the earliest of times. Confusion arises, however, in the attribution of vowels and pitches. Everyone argues furiously about this, instead of actually getting on and doing something practical.

Let us, therefore, consider one working method allocating Vowels to the Elements.

## Vowels, from Earth to Air

There is an inherent Elemental resonance in the Four Vowels A, E, I, and O: it is concerned with qualities or nodal energies. The order of Elemental spiralling is A  O  I  E, from the most open or slowest vowel, to the most tense active or rapid vowel. A/ Earth, O/ Water, I/  Fire, E/  Air. When uttering tones or calls for the Elements, this order of vowels is very effective, due to the deep affinity between the nature of the vowel concerned and the appropriate Element that it declares.

## Breath, Voice, Overtones

The human voice is our most effective means of musical empowerment. The reasons for this are numerous, and open to a number of different 'explanations', but the root of the power of voice is that it is our ultimate vehicle for expression of entity, of consciousness, of Being. Traditional cosmologies frequently describe Creation, the first appearance of Being, as an utterance, a Voice, a Word; and Breath is always associated with the originative Spirit. Humanity is a reflection, a harmonic, a miniature of the universal Being. Thus our breath, our voice, and our physical organism hold within them the mirror of the creation and formation of the universe.

We do not need to accept this ancient teaching as religion or dogma of any sort; there is ample evidence of the power of voice that withstands even the most stringent materialist analysis. The power of voice is recognized, for example, in various branches of speech and music therapy, without any well-defined theory or rules of practice being established. Such theory and disciplines, however, were highly developed in the ancient world, remain in use within certain schools of religious and magical singing even today, and may be restated for contemporary practice. There are, however, a number of significant differences between the use of voice for inner transformation and general skill at singing, or the power of instrumental music.

The most important asset of the human voice is that it acts directly upon the physical organism in some very distinct ways, which have been the subject of study and practice for many thousands of years in magical and spiritual disciplines around the world. The results of this art of empowered voice may be heard *not* in classical music or opera, but in liturgical chant or plainsong, shamanistic chants, epic magical narrative singing, temple chants throughout the East, and in the truly immense protean collection of ritual chanting that permeates all cultures worldwide.

Remnants of such ritual chanting are even found in Britain in outlying areas such as the west of Ireland, the Scottish Highlands and islands, and many isolated regions of north-western Europe. Wherever such anonymous traditional magical chants or calls occur, they are, of course, coloured by the ethnic music of the people and region that they represent. But there are some definable aspects to this type of singing that clearly separate it from art song or even general folksong and popular entertainment.

So on one hand we have the specific training of the priest, priestess, magician, or mystic in the empowered use of voice to alter consciousness, and on the other we have a collective anonymous body of singing, song-lore and poems, and folk rituals, the substance of which often seems to endure through time, reaching back into very deep cultural roots.

Although we have suggested here a specific inner art to the use of voice in connection with energies and consciousness, it has its spontaneous outer manifestations in the natural jubilations or ululations found in primal cultures. We shall return to this concept in more detail shortly, but it is sufficient at this stage to state that this natural vocalization was closely observed by the early Fathers of the Christian Church, and that they deliberately adopted its forms for early liturgical use in worship. This natural vocal form, which must have varied from region to region, combined with the arts of chant inherited from pagan temples, led to the development of plainchant, which went through a number of forms prior to those still in limited use today.[13]

Direct action of voice upon the organism occurs if we listen to empowered singing or chanting, which is not necessarily identical to operatically trained or highly artistic singing. It can, under certain circumstances, be far more effective than instrumental music, which also has a direct effect upon the organism in various ways. The voice is at its most powerful as an empowering vehicle, however, when it is deliberately used for that purpose; our own voices, either alone or in group work, have a highly complex empowering, rejuvenating, and elevating effect.

When the consciousness of the singer or singers is truly attuned to potent inner levels, to modes of awareness that are usually excluded or rejected, this change of consciousness is communicated by the voice. It can, under certain circumstances, trigger a resonant response in listeners. This is the whole principle of liturgical or magical chant. It is not, however, merely a matter of 'emotions', such as are communicated in opera or romantic song, or in highly emotional religious singing. We are concerned with both Elemental and spiritual levels in empowered voice, and emotions alone are insufficient, and may even be distracting or severely limiting in terms of inner development. The entire concept of balance between emotions and other energies is discussed in Chapters 9 and 10 where we examine the musical potential of the Axis Mundi and the Tree of Life, which are universal models of perception and energy.

It must be emphasized here that empowered vocalization is not a matter of 'good' singing or musical skill, for musical ability or vocal quality is, for the greater part, irrelevant.

There is a further dimension to this transformative power of voice, for even the most ugly of voices can and does eventually transform through the applied use of empowered vocalization, chant, and imagination. The voice, therefore, transforms itself. The key to such transformation is not simply in technique, discipline or persistence, though these are, of course essential. It lies in the use of imaginative forces, and the attuning of the Elemental energies within one's self. These harmonized forces cause the transformation, and without them, nothing is possible.

The potential of vocal flowering may, of course, be limited by physical problems such as disability or damage: many voices, for example, are ruined for ever by so-called 'training'. Polluted atmospheres, and addictions such as smoking, cause widespread catarrh, congestion of the sinuses and related ear, nose, and throat ailments throughout Western society and in industrial and city-based societies worldwide. This second area of vocal limitation can gradually be reduced through breathing exercises and vocal use, for healthier breathing habits and the disciplines of daily vocalizing go a long way towards revitalizing the respiratory system. The overall health will benefit too, once the voice has been liberated and the true energizing potential of the breath has begun to develop.

## The Power of Voice

Let us examine the simple but profound traditions concerning voice, which are based upon the relationships between physics and metaphysics, imagination and magic, spirit and body.

The perennial spiritual, cosmological traditions repeatedly affirm that the universe is made of music: music is simply defined as sound in proportional patterns. These proportions, which hold good regardless of size or relative scale, for they may be upon a stellar scale or a cellular or atomic scale, are reiterated in many of the patterns discernible by modern science. These same patterns in varying presentation were defined by earlier artistic sciences or magic through specific symbols, poetic and mythic sequences, and through some of the unusual mathematical or geometric and topological or morphological theories connected to entities such as the Platonic solids. The Tree of Life, which has a close relationship to the Platonic Solids and the Pythagorean Tetractys, is usually published as a flat glyph or map, which harmonizes relationships between the stellar, solar, and planetary entities and energies. Such glyphs are always flat representations of spherical models (see Figures 5 and 6).

The truths of modern physics and mathematics are merely restatements of such conceptual models; not merely theoretical models, but practical expositions of concepts drawn from inner perceptions gained through listening to the universal proportions in meditation.

The foundations of modern astronomy were laid exactly in such a manner by Johannes Kepler in the sixteenth and seventeenth centuries. He commenced as a young man with a vision, in which relationship between the Five Regular Solids revealed to him the proportions of the heliocentric system and the orbits of the planets. By 1596 his work *The*

Figure 8

# Vowels Chants and Elements

The four vowel sounds E-I-O-A declare and relate to the Four Elements. The highest and most complex or active vowel sound is *Eee* and the lowest and least active vowel sound is *Aaa*. The rising and falling vowels are associated with levels of pitch connected to the Elements. In primal magical utterance of power-tones, these do not require a selected or modern series of musical notes, providing AIR or Eee is the highest, and EARTH or Aaa is the lowest.

In ancient magical utterances, the vowel sounds were elided and combined in a sliding or chromatic sequence of pitch, with no clearly defined scale or mode or steps between. Primal chanting of vowels and raising and lowering of pitch connected to Elemental energies is a very powerful exercise.

The use of Vowels in connection with the Four Elements is at the root of speech and consciousness: in many mystical or magical systems the vowels are regarded as particularly sacred, for they give the spirit to any word. Words cannot be uttered without vowels, just as the manifest entities of the universe cannot exist without the empowering Elements or spiritual Being uttering through them.

```
High
 Eee→AIR      4
 Iii→FIRE     3
Ooo→WATER     2
Aaa→EARTH     1
 Low
```

| I | 4 | 2 | 3 |
|---|---|---|---|
| 4 | 3 | I | 2 |
| 2 | I | 3 | 4 |
| 3 | 2 | 4 | I |

Elemental Square as Numbers

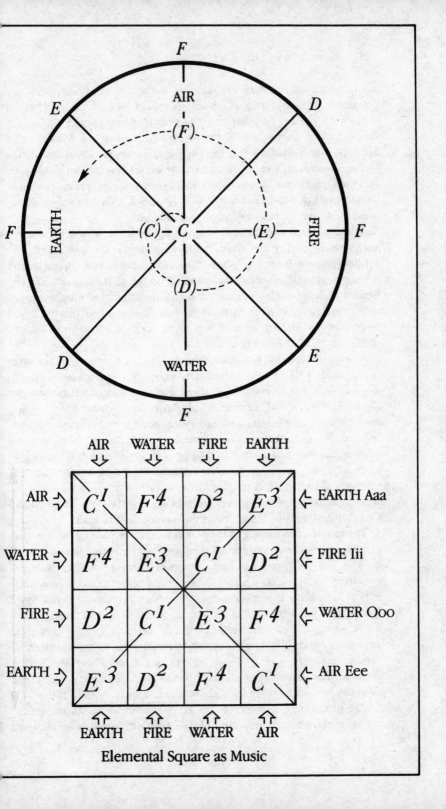

Elemental Square as Music

*Cosmographical Mystery* showed that the proportions were not only geometric, but harmonic, which simply means musical. By 1619 he had written his famous *Five Books on Cosmic Harmony*, which included a mathematical restatement of the ancient concept of the Music of the Spheres, a polyphonic set of relationships. Through subsequent mathematical research, Kepler stated three laws of planetary motion which laid the foundations for modern rationalist cosmogony; yet his discovery came out of dedication to a spiritual revelation that has only recently been rediscovered: that the universe is musical.

While rational science has tended to apply direct laws of number to such concepts, they are actually found in nature through spiral logarithmic sets; these are reflected in organic entities, and appear within ourselves in various forms, including the shape of the human ear. The genetic code, recently evaluated and still the subject of much research and experiment, is nothing more or less than a set of rotations and combinations of four units. So modern biology restates the ancient model of the Four Elements.

In esoteric tradition the principle of resonance, harmony, and octaves is frequently applied as an unstated foundation to techniques. Thus the Tree of Life, which consists of three triads or sets of harmonies (see Figure 5), three spirals of relationship, in which each turn of the spiral reiterates certain energies and harmonies upon a higher level, may not be directly applicable to precise mathematics. But visualization and musical chants or patterns based upon such models lead, nevertheless, to an inner response. The detailed mathematics may never be stated, as in mystical and magical training, or may be the work of a lifetime, as with Johannes Kepler. It is the resonant response to the primary model that is important, for it permeates through our entire entity.

The music or elemental chant that is used for willed transformation of consciousness and of physical energies works through sets of relative laws. These laws may be stated in various ways, but they underpin existence nevertheless. This is an important matter that is frequently overlooked: *there are many ways to state the protean universal laws*. No single rigid definition, statement or model is correct. Regrettably, many writers on esoteric subjects, music included, have a very rigid attitude, perhaps deriving from the infantile need to be reassured by concretized systems. It is the living practice of empowerment that is essential, not assembling sets of theories and reassuring oneself that these (and these only) are the right method, laws or rules to follow.

The proportions concerned are apprehended by us as music, for music displays certain relationships, shapes, and intervals or apparent 'distances' between selected tones or utterances. Such distances, usually defined as higher or lower notes, are really a matter of relative rates of vibration. This attraction towards proportions is inherent within human consciousness, and although traditions of music vary worldwide, they have more than sufficient in common to prove that certain proportions seem to be inherent to our perception. Disastrously, Western art and commercial music reflects certain mechanistic limitations within our society, for many of the major attributes of natural music have been wilfully ironed out, removed or discarded. Such limitation and arbitrary emasculation of aspects of music does not, however, dispose of them in nature, or upon our deepest levels of consciousness and organic or biological perception and reaction.

When discussing music, Westerners often state, quite incorrectly, that intervals found in non-Western music, such as the quarter or eighth tone, and the varied thirds and sevenths of ethnic scales or modes, show distinct differences of musical awareness between West and East, or between white and black musical consciousness, and so forth. In art music, the use of intervals of less than one semitone, or untempered scales or scales of varying temperament, are regarded as wildly experimental or exotic.

All such comparative, separatist speculation on world musics is nonsense. We need only to listen to the ethnic musics of the West to hear an abundance of intervals less than a semitone, to hear scales that have three or more choices for intervals such as the third, the second, the seventh, and so forth. Such subtlety was ironed out of art music within the narrow confines of patronage and court, but remained almost untouched for centuries in folk music and song. It is on this level that the collective traditional music of the West relates to the great spiritual and classical musics of the East, which have never lost their foundation in collective musical consciousness and style.

The current trend of increased awareness of 'World Music', despite its gross commercialization and trivialization, is an important step in the reopening of Western musical consciousness to the proportions of nature, the land, the universe. But it does not, by any means, suggest that such proportions are missing from Western musical consciousness and that they have to be sought in Africa or the East; the current reopening is effective precisely because these sounds, the subtle rhythms, the small intervals, the organic or holistic style of collective music, reawaken part of our own consciousness which has been closed by rigid art music or by commercial pop. In other words we respond to world music because we partake of it, it is within us. Music is a matter of proportion, of relationship, of relative motion and position in time and space, of rates of vibration, of energy, of pattern.

The same proportions are now being rediscovered in sciences such as genetics and physics, and on the frontiers of mathematics. We say rediscovered, for the ancient theories ascribed to Pythagoras and Plato, and the related esoteric traditions of magical music and cosmology, have long affirmed that certain proportions hold good throughout all worlds. In nature we find the logarithmic spiral of expansion and contraction, which has a musical analogy; in the solar system we have the proportion of the planetary orbits; in the universe we have the proportionality of the stars and their immense energies and movements, best known through the awe-inspiring swirling of nebulae. And of course such relative movements are reflected upon an atomic scale. Wherever we research, listen or look, relative proportion creates distinctive patterns, and the patterns relate, regardless of physical scale or size.

Thus the universe is made of music: sound, which is to say energy, in proportional patterns of various categories, with many clear relationships between the categories. Our advancing sciences merely discover more information concerning such relationships; the knowledge of the relationships themselves has always been present within us.

The entire subject, or perhaps we should say *reality*, of proportion is found in music through harmonics. Harmonics are defined proportions which occur naturally when a tone is uttered or generated. When the human voice utters, it may seem to generate one single note or tone, but in fact a multitude of proportions, harmonics, and partials or overtones are present in the sound. This fact of nature, this physical reality, is at the root of all metaphysics and magic involving music. Indeed, the tone uttered, or the shape of a chant or melody as sung, is considered to be less important than the overtones or apparently unperceived harmonics. These harmonics are the proportions that arouse our subtle energies, that open our awareness to metaphysical or transpersonal proportions and states of consciousness, which traditionally are known as worlds or as entities, beings that resonate in harmony with us, if we are able to gain contact with them.

## Overtones

Overtone singing has become rather fashionable in recent years, often taken out of its proper magical or meditational context. The physical and metaphysical principles behind overtone utterance are central to traditions of empowerment and transformation through music, and the current trend of overtone singing is the merest beginning of a general restatement of music that will expand into the twenty-first century.

At present the utterance of overtones is a rather refined gimmick for most Westerners, a technique whereby more than one note may be sung at once, or by which exotic sounds may be generated. While classes and commercial records of overtone singing have gained a growing popularity, they are almost without exception not presented as part of a dedicated discipline or way of life, and are generally separated from any cultural or spiritual organic tradition. Of course, we might add that such fragmentation is typical of most aspects of contemporary culture, and that we might find it in any number of other examples if we choose to search for it.

As a venerable technique connected to spiritual and magical arts, examples of overtone singing are found in Tibetan tantric chanting, shamanistic or magical chant among primal peoples worldwide, certain ancient liturgies of the Christian Church, and in very precise disciplines and vocal arts taught to members of highly dedicated mystical, magical or esoteric orders.

The basis of overtone utterance, however, is rooted in nature: when we emit a tone, many others are inherent and alive within it. Specific vocal techniques enable these inherent notes to become increasingly recognizable. The implications of this simple acoustic phenomenon are this: the apparent tone, note or event is in fact only one facet or part of a holism. It is, therefore, a reflection of the universe in the human voice.

The appearance of high partials or overtones is traditionally regarded as proof of the presence of spirit within the physical voice; high pitches are often associated with higher entities or forces. But paradoxically, we raise such forces by uttering very low chants or empowered tones. Usually three levels of pitch are employed – corresponding to the Three Worlds: the low voice, the middle or customary voice, and the overtone or high voice.

# 13   Colour, Scales, Music

We now come to the subject of colour, which has been widely developed and exploited in recent years. If we examine the range of modern literature on colour therapy, and the relationship between colour and sound or colour and music, it soon becomes clear that there is little firm agreement between writers and practitioners. Basic colour therapy and basic colour enhancement of surroundings seem to have gained a general consensus during the last 20 years or so, but the deeper level of esoteric magical or spiritual arts relating to colour, and the relationship between sound, music, and colour, remains in a state of total confusion.

The origins of a fusion between sound and colour are simple to establish historically: we have an early reference in Plato's *Myth of Er*, (see Appendix 3), an instructional Mystery tale found in *The Republic*, written in the fourth century BC. Here certain shapes, colours, and musical tones are related together in a cosmological vision: the colour progression is that of the colours of the planets of the solar system, with a band of chromatic colour reserved for the stellar universe.

We may therefore accurately state that sound and colour were being linked in terms of planetary force and bodies at least 3,000 years ago. We know that many early civilizations atttributed colours to planetary divinities and forces, and that this direct system was inherited by diffuse magical and Mystery sects and orders. The classical system of the ancient world persisted in an attenuated form through the Dark and Middle Ages, particularly in the underground traditions of esoteric learning.

In the Renaissance, there was a considerable revival of attributing colours and tones to planetary entities, gods and goddesses, and energies. These were, more or less, restatements and refinements of the inheritance of the ancient world. The systems were poetic and mythic, founded in simple observation of planetary hues in the night sky, and upon the qualities, mythic activities, and planetary energies or forces associated with classical deities. They relied as much upon mystical tradition as upon observation.

This is the same colour and tone system that persisted in various forms into the eighteenth and nineteenth centuries, when scientific advances enabled the study of colour to become more precise. The basic spectrum of colours of the rainbow had been known since ancient times, and had been restated by medieval and Renaissance alchemists (the forerunners of physicists and scientists) and philosophers.

The relationship between colours, psychic energies, health, and musical tones, however, became confused by pseudo-scientific applications and theories, mainly those published by the Theosophical Society and taken up by almost every spiritualist and magical or meditational group from the nineteenth century onwards. We repeatedly find in Theosophical and spiritualist literature, and in the teachings of strictly magical orders such as the Hermetic Order of the Golden Dawn, that certain colours correspond to certain energies and musical tones. Regrettably, we are also told that the system as published or taught 'by the Masters' contained blinds, substitutions, and intentional changes, as the truth was simply 'too powerful' for the general public.

This nonsense persists in the later writings of magical orders in the twentieth century, with much waffling and burbling regarding complementary colours, colours that change when seen upon the inner planes and so forth.

What all of the foregoing comes down to is, regrettably, that no one knew what they were doing. The revolutionary fusion of precise traditions from the East, in the form of Hindu and Buddhist mystical teachings (essential as a corrective force to the constipated and corrupted religion of the West in the nineteenth century), with the old classical systems with which they share much in common might have been possible, but seems to have failed dismally. One possible reason for this failure is that it was too intellectual, too much of a mental synthesis without a collective readiness or deep change of real awareness; even today, at the close of the twentieth century, that change of awareness has not fully occurred. Another possible reason was the mad rush to 'justify' occult theories, already confused and juxtaposed with one another, in terms of modern mathematics, physics, psychology, and other developing sciences. The result: confusion.

In the twentieth century there has been some significant research into the psychology of colour, and into the relationships between vibratory rates of colour and (octave-related) vibratory rates of music. The scientific answer must, surely, be found by such methods.

But for practical work with energies and consciousness a simple, direct set of colours and tones is needed, and this has always existed with a few basic variants. All the superficially profound and mysterious nonsense about colours astrally complementing one another and changing vibratory rates to the inner perception is, in its own way, true, but it is a matter of experience rather than description, and cannot be limited to a written teaching that simply serves to misdirect the student away from direct effective work.

## Colour and Sound: A Statement of the Obvious

Before examining a working variant of the traditional colour system, I would like to make a statement: there is no requirement that we link musical utterance and colour at all. Why try to intellectually align that which our consciousness resolves in any case?

If we carry this seeking after correspondences too far, it becomes an obsessive and time-wasting project: is my room the right colour? Should I play a piano piece by Satie or perhaps a tape of the Aka pygmy chant, and which one will clash with the inherent tones in my aura? Is my green meditation robe astrally red or blue when I chant a vowel sound on the pitch B-flat? And on and on. . . .

The answer is always, but always, to be found in simplicity and directness. Anything that is not organically or holistically clear is a waste of time and energy. Such holisms are established and perpetuated in two basic ways. The first is through perennial tradition, which must, despite its inherent value, be amended according to individual needs. The second is through intuition, which is greatly enhanced by meditation and stillness. Our intuition should be applied to a teaching tradition, just as the tradition helps develop our inner faculties by its preservation and dissemination of techniques.

It may be that dedicated mathematicians and psychologists, working with computer models, will come up with increasingly refined and workable maps of the relationships between musical vibration, colour, and psychic states.[18] But as soon as they do so, new thresholds will be found, and variants will appear. Such is the nature of the universe, the fullness: it cannot be rigidly defined, only harmonically reflected and modulated. Why should our human psychic entity, a mirror of the universe, be any different?

## Colour, Tones, and the Elements

*A cautionary note*

Before discussing colour and musical relationship within a basic Elemental system, one of the standard warnings has to be given: it applies to us all, in varying degrees. There is a basic human weakness, an elemental imbalance, variably inherent in each of us. The actual relationship between Elements in any individual is seldom properly balanced, but the degree of imbalance varies from person to person and from phase to phase in a life cycle.

One typical form that this weakness takes appears frequently in meditation and visualization, and it consists of the well-known and addictive habit of astral-tripping. I have deliberately used a modern slang term, originating with the use of LSD, for this weakness, rather than say psychotropic fantasy or kaleidoscopic reveries. What it comes down to is the visualizer's equivalent of watching television; entering an inner state and watching the colours flow and change. It must be emphasized that this can be a highly addictive habit, and difficult for some people to shake off. Many psychic hobbies are astral television, and little more, but the very trivia of it all is potentially dangerous.

One of the most balanced methods of avoiding this trip habit is in a fusion of activities: sound, movement, colour, and imagery. The dedication and alignment of Sacred Space, attuned to the Four Elements, sets our energies into a cycle of motion, and at a later stage into a harmonized relationship; this is the key to inner transformation and empowerment. The exercises in our next chapter are designed to work towards such a balance.

The following information, therefore, deals with colours and colour changes in relationship to musical tones, but such visualizations must always form part of a disciplined work programme, and not be idle colour-trips.

The Four Elements traditionally have a number of related colours. For practical purposes we should keep this set of relationships simple: in advanced work each group or student will find that they commence with chosen colours attuned to an Elemental pitch or Call, but that the colours will transform as the energies themselves transform and interact. This colour change could be as simple as an intensifying of the colour chosen for visualization or as dramatic as a complete change through the spectrum. Perhaps the most comprehensive method of working with colours is to visualize the Sacred Space (see Figure 5), with an appropriate landscape for each Quarter (Spring, Summer, Autumn, Winter). This will, of itself, generate certain colour responses. These will transform through the intensity of the Elemental Chants or Calls, described in our next chapter.

It is possible to develop the concentration to such an extent that pure colours are used, either alone or in association with musical tones. This is one of the most ancient training exercises for consciousness, and may be further refined by visualization of certain solids or geometric shapes, which may be of a single colour, or of increasingly complex colour relationships upon their facets, planes, or delineations.

The Tree of Life is such an image, and originally used only the traditional planetary colours – features which probably appeared upon the Tree of Life no earlier than the Renaissance. During the eighteenth and nineteenth centuries, a number of 'colour scales' were applied to the Tree of Life, with little or no reference to Kabbalistic tradition, and mainly drawn from crude summaries of Eastern colour teachings, wrenched from their proper religious, mystical, and cultural context. All of this should be left strictly alone unless you are willing to spend a very long period of intellectual effort and library research, time which could well be spent meditating upon the Four Elements and traditional Planetary Colours and their resonance within the human energy field or power centres.

Here is one basic colour and tonal (musical) scale that works effectively:

EARTH   Black/   Planet Earth/   Fundamental or starting note (C)
WATER   Silver/   The Moon/   Second note (D)
FIRE   Gold/   The Sun/   Third note (E)
AIR   Crystalline (Clear)/   Fourth note (F)

This colour sequence is the Earth or Mineral colour scale. It uses metallic or crystalline colours that are fundamentally associated in our consciousness with the Four Elements and the Axis Mundi or World Pivot of Earth–Moon–Sun–Star. It also attunes to the energies of the Four Power Centres of *Feet*, *Genitals*, *Heart*, and *Throat* or *Head*. The energy rate of each colour or tone is 'raised' through each relative Element, though this may be taken mythically or poetically just as much as in terms of numerical vibrations of the wavelengths.

It should be clear from the above, and from the associated tables and diagrams in our exercises, that an Elemental single tone could be uttered while visualizing a colour, while arousing the related Power Centre or chakra, and while attuning in meditation to the Planetary World of force concerned. This in itself is not quite as difficult as it seems in printed description, for all of these apparently separated entities are in fact harmonic expressions of one another in different octaves.

We might then use the Elemental calls (see page 141) and visualize a colour change according to each note, giving a rapid sequence of flashing colours.

A second basic colour scale could be used as follows:

EARTH   Green (and all plant hues)
WATER   Blue (and all sea hues)
FIRE    Red (and all flame hues)
AIR     White (and all sky hues)

This might be termed the organic or environmental colour scale.

## The Tree of Life and Planetary Colours

The direct colour system of the Tree of Life, excluding nineteenth-century literary variants, as mentioned briefly above, is closely related to the old planetary colours known and taught at least as early as Ancient Greece and Egypt. (Refer to Figure 5 for the basic glyph and the relationship of colours to one another.)

1: Clear   2: Rainbow or Silver Grey (swirling of all colours)   3: Deep Black.

These are the cosmic or universal supernal colours: the Crown, First Utterance or Primum Mobile; the Stars or Zodiac; Saturn, the Great Mother Deep.

4: Sky Blue   5: Blood Red   6: Bright Golden Yellow

These are the Solar or clearly polarized colours: Jupiter, the Giver; Mars, the Taker; Sun, the Harmonizer.

7: Brilliant Green   8: Orange   9: Purple or Violet

These are the Lunar or mixed colours: Venus, goddess of the feelings; Mercury, god of the intellect; the Moon, goddess of fertility, birth and death (i.e. Blue + Yellow = Green/ Red + Yellow = Orange/ Red + Blue = Purple or Violet).

10: Four Earth colours, usually Brown, Black, Dark Green, and Orange Yellow.

These represent the cycle of the Four Seasons, and the Four Elements upon planet Earth divided a circle into Four Quarters.

It can be seen that the colours have an Orange to Red to Black range on one polarity, the catabolic Spheres or Planets, and a Green to Blue to Rainbow range on the opposite or anabolic polarity. The central pivot of the Three Worlds rotates around Clear, Yellow Gold, or Violet Purple.

In a short space we have defined three colour scales which could be used in work with appropriate musical tone or Elemental calls. They are the Mineral, the Environmental, and the Planetary or Cosmic colour scale. There is enough in this triple colour scale alone to last any of us a lifetime of inner work in meditation, visualization and spiritual realization.

# 14  Elemental Calls
in Three Worlds:
A training programme

There are Four levels to the Spiral of the Elements; each level corresponds in itself to an Element. The four levels are Earth, Water, Fire, and Air. They ascend in a continuous spiral, turning through a cycle of one octave for each level. Thus Earth is the most substantial or materialized Element within a relative set of Four Elements, while Air is the least substantial and most mobile Element within a relative set of Four Elements. In this spiralling of octaves, we reach from the lowest audible level within our hearing to the highest, from Earth to Air. This will give us a range of seven octaves, though this range is by no means the limit of sound vibrations, nor is it the limit of sound vibrations that actually affect the human organism and consciousness.

Due to the universal law of octaves, however, we can work very well within our audible range of seven octaves, and indeed, can work with Elemental Music within a much smaller range without impairing its potency in any way. One octave, in terms of elemental calls or musical glyphs, stands for all, and the first four intervals in an octave scale or mode, its first half, stand for the second four, and vice versa.

This reduction of octaves works due to the action of harmonics, or partials, by which any selected pitch has mirrored or inherent within its other notes in certain strict universal proportions. In our basic Elemental circle, we allocate the notes as follows: C = Earth/ D = Water/ E = Fire/ F = Air. This fourfold ascending pattern is one half of the modern Western scale, one half of the octave (see Figure 8). The second half is inherent within these four notes, for G is the fifth note above C, and is a *harmonic,* an overtone or partial of C. We cannot utter C, either with the voice or an instrument, without the presence of other notes as overtones and, more obscurely, undertones. The fifth (see Figure 2) is a prime overtone, in the proportion 3:1. This emerges from the very simple diverging series of 1:1 (any first pitched utterance); 2:1, the octave 'twice as high', which is physically and inwardly recognizable by us all; 3:1, the fifth note of the scale, perhaps the first type of harmony used, as its harmonic overtone tends frequently to break through into a full audible identity.

The most prominent overtones that come alive from a fundamental tone are usually the octave, a third, the fifth, and a seventh of a scale. I say 'a third' and 'a seventh' because they are not necessarily the two types of third and seventh steps found on modern instruments, but are those inherent in the proportions of nature. By comparison with a modern keyboard they would sound flat to the major seventh or third, and sharp to the minor seventh and third, but in their own right they are extremely satisfying intervals, particularly when uttered by the human voice, which inherently produces these overtones and intervals. In many ethnic musics, in both the East and West, we find use of three third steps of a scale or mode, and three sevenths. Even today, the traditional Irish uilleann bagpipes, to take what might be considered to be an unlikely example, as they are in widespread and popular use, have at least three readily distinguishable and playable sevenths to their basic scale (either founded upon D, C, or more rarely B or B flat), three readily distinguishable thirds, and on some older and highly refined instruments from the last century (plus a few good modern instruments) a well-defined super-sharpened octave, with a quite specific fingering and use in the traditional repertoire, distinct from the proper octave. All of these variable notes are used to great and fully conscious effect by players, who are drawing upon an old, microtonal tradition.

The Elemental Calls commence for us, as humans upon the planet, in the Earth mode. A complete simple cycle of the Four Elements, from Earth to Air, spirals through C D E F. A further harmonic of that simple rotation is G A B C. This brings us again to C, but it is C 2:1 above our starting C, or one octave. It also utters as the Element of Air, one entire octave above the Element of Earth. Thus our first cycle has uttered Earth of Earth/   Water of Earth/   Fire of Earth/   Air of Earth. The notes are: C + G/   D + A/   E + B/   F + C. The C is usually our lowest vocal note, and not necessarily a keyboard C.

We need to spiral an entire octave of octaves before C utters as the Element of Earth again. This octave of octaves is the limit of human hearing and completes the cycle of Elements and overtones.

There are two simple ways of approaching this expanding spiral of octaves in a mapped form: one is as a flat or 'horizontal' circle (see Figure 2), the other is as a flat but 'vertical' line, really the axis or central pivot of the ascending spiral (see Figure 6). In reality, the two graphic axes – vertical and horizontal – are convenient ways of showing on paper that which really must be uttered and heard. Its reality is in sound, not on paper, just as a map of a region is not the region itself.

The lowest octave and full Elemental Cycle, is composed of all Four Elements, the notes C–C, and reaches from Earth to Air in an ascending scale. We may utter the first four notes, C D E F, or all eight notes, C D E F G A B C. This is the Earth World corresponding to our Planet Earth and all associated energies and entities, and to the power centre and zone of the Feet (see Figure 4). This is the Earth Mode, which broadly corresponds to the scale of C major on a modern keyboard, though the actual planetary pitch of the commencing C is somewhat lower than that used in art music today. This note is learned orally by musicians in India, and may also occur in the low 'C' drone pitches used in Western ethnic musics, such as those of various bagpipes.

The next level or turn of the spiral commences again at Earth, but its first note is in the octave above our original starting note of C for Earth, and furthermore utters as the note D, one tone above the final C of the Earth cycle (see Figure 2). This is the Lunar World, corresponding to the Moon and all associated energies and entities, and to the power centre and zone of the Genitals. Once again we turn through a complete Elemental Cycle and octave, but it is now the Water or Lunar Mode (D–D). Thus it utters Earth of Water, Water of Water, Fire of Water, Air of Water. The notes are D + A/ E + B/ F + C/ G + D. We are now beginning to discover the simple modality of an Elemental Cycle or Spiral. All Elements are always present, but their relative relationships change through the octaves, through the Worlds.

The third level or turn of the spiral commences again in the Quarter and Element of Earth, but now upon the note E, one tone above the final note of the Lunar Mode. This is the Solar World, corresponding to the Sun (Solar System) and all associated energies and entities. It resonates with the power centre and zone of the Heart in the human organism, and stretches for an entire octave, E–E, the Solar Mode. The notes are E + B/ F + C/ G + D/ A + E.

The fourth level of the spiral, again commencing in the Element of Earth, begins and ends on F, ascending through one octave. This is the Stellar World, corresponding to the Stars (of which our Sun is one) and all associated energies and entities. In the Human organism it resonates with the power centre and zone of the Head, and utters as the notes one octave, F–F, the Stellar Mode. The notes are therefore F + C/ G + D/ A + E/ B + F.

In modern musical terms, this last F is required to become an F# (sharp) if it is to give a perfect fifth to the B. The expansion and contraction of fifths throughout the spiralling octaves was originally used to demonstrate cyclical or spherical infinite expansion of the universe; modern tempering and adjustment tends to obscure this expansion, tidying-up intervals to make a neat workable keyboard for the pianist. The tidying process, tempering, of which several versions have been available since ancient times, applies in various ways to all Western musical instruments, particularly when they play together.

In ethnic musics and Eastern classical and folk musics, this problem hardly arises, as the basis of the music is often microtonal and always modal. I would stress that microtonality and complex modality is as much part of European ethnic music as of oriental music, but regrettably, the rift between art and collective music became so wide that microtonal concepts were finally recognized in folk music only towards the close of the nineteenth century and in the early years of the twentieth, by which time much of the vast inheritance of European ethnic music had already been destroyed.

## A Training Programme for Elemental Calls

A basic training programme in empowered vocalizing is simple to follow: the constituents are not complicated or obscure, and build from very ordinary foundations without technical vocabulary or pseudo-mystical jargon. Such simplicity does not alter the fact that teachings of the type described in our training programme have been in use for thousands of years; the ambience of culture and the language employed, of course, will change from time to time and place to place, but the basics of human energy, breath, voice, and the Elements remain.

The initial stages of this training require careful repetition and regular application; this type of training, like any other, builds through regular use. Idle experimentation is fruitless, but careful repeated effort, combined with patience, will bring distinct and powerful results.

The following programme of training may be easily self-administered, or may be undertaken by a group of people working together. If the second option is followed, there should also be some individual work at home, not only to build upon and reinforce group training, but to ensure that the group does not become the sole source of inner work, possibly creating a false dependence.

The different units within the programme may also be worked with in their own right at a later stage and upon more advanced levels, but the basic sequence of training and development must be established first.

As a general rule the basic units outlined should be worked with until they are familiar and natural, before any of the advanced stages are tried. Such familiarity and naturalization will take a minimum of two to three months, and a full cycle of each stage outlined below could take a year from beginning to end, and then continue as a regular discipline for the rest of a lifetime.

For reference purposes, a general suggested timescale is included with each stage or exercise, but different people will learn and develop at different rates, so it is not to be considered as a rule or an inevitable pattern. Much of the pacing of inner disciplines becomes, with long practice, a matter of intuition, but the intuition and self-pacing cannot develop until a firm foundation of very strict, disciplined training has been laid down. Without this essential hard work and discipline in the early stages, there is nothing for the intuition to work with, no established patterns either as physical training or in the way of inner growth. Traditionally, a personal teacher is present to assess the points of transition, to suggest or define when the pupil may move on into higher or deeper aspects of training. Today we are not able to work in this manner, so each stage is laid out as a simple overall plan of self-training.

## Breathing the Four Directions
### (*the first month*)

This exercise is best done out of doors, or before open windows in fresh air. The fresh air rule applies throughout all empowered vocal work, though at much later stages it may be necessary to work indoors in seclusion with advanced visualizing techniques.

All the usual basic rules of meditation apply, such as wearing loose, comfortable clothing, working in a situation where no sudden disturbance will occur, and ensuring careful attention and concentration upon each phase of the exercise. This is not, essentially, a course of physical training in the sense of a sport, of keeping fit, or of muscular development. Although we use the voice, it is not a type of vocal training in the sense of artistic endeavour, though it will help natural expansion and beauty of voice considerably in the long term. It is a holism, a harmonic programme of work which combines physical and inner training; by this method false barriers between inner and outer energy and expression, between the vital forces, the imagination and the body, are gradually broken down and realigned constructively.

If you are addicted to tobacco the preliminary breathing and balancing exercises may help you towards a cure, but empowered vocal work cannot progress beyond the most basic levels if you smoke. The choice is simple: if you wish to work with empowered voice and chant, you must give up your addiction. If you cannot do this, you are too ineffectual for this type of inner development.

By way of balance we should add that non-smokers will also have any number of addictions and habits that come to the fore as barriers to inner development; there is no 'value' judgement as to one addiction or negative habit being any worse or better than another. As we are concerned here with breath and vocal tones, however, smoking is the most prevalent weakness and addiction that interferes with or counter-acts progress and empowerment.

In spiritual and magical development, the weaknesses or imbalances are seen as feedback patterns between the Elemental energies of the individual; they are like knots or tangles which absorb life energy and divert it away from proper routes, from harmony and balance. If they can be unravelled and reassigned in a more balanced pattern, these convoluted self-amplifying nodes of elemental energy are tremendously valuable and effective sources of power. Training exercises such as the detailed programme described here can go a long way towards lessening the hold of habits and negative tendencies, but the will to change must come from the individual.

Let us now return to the breathing exercises themselves, either out-doors or in a well-ventilated room.

Some simple deep breathing may be done while standing or sitting to clear the lungs. No special techniques should be practised during this warm-up, as they will interfere with what is to follow. If you have already learned yoga breathing exercises or similar techniques, you will need to clear your mind down to the very simplest basics of healthy breathing, and absolutely nothing more. Mixing techniques is a waste of time and energy, and, in some (admittedly rare) circumstances, can be debilitating or even potentially dangerous to health and psychic balance.

a)  Stand upright with arms raised to a horizontal position. Empty your lungs by breathing out using the diaphragm to expel as much air as possible. As you expel the air, gently lower your arms to your sides.

b)  Breathe in steadily through the nose (mouth closed, tongue touching the roof of the mouth just behind the teeth). As you breathe in, raise the arms steadily, and rise on to your toes. This may take a little practice initially, so if you lose your balance, simply breathe out and begin again.

c)  With arms held out horizontally, expel the breath through your mouth, counting quietly aloud '1-2-3-4' and lower your feet and arms together to the position of rest.

This is the outer or preliminary form of the exercise. Several levels of inner work are added to it as you progress, the first being brought into operation as soon as you can draw breath and rise on to your toes and remain balanced for the minimum of four to eight seconds necessary. As you develop breath and balance, this period will lengthen naturally, but it should never be a feat of endurance or a self-imposed trial. There is always a natural limit and period to such breathing and balancing, and this begins as a fairly short period, and gradually lengthens. Striving is counterproductive.

## Breathing the Directions
*(within the first month, extending well into the second month)*

The first breath out, quietly uttered as '1' is defined by focusing awareness before you. The second breath is defined by focusing awareness to your right; the third behind you, and the fourth to your left. When this circular focusing or orientation has been completed, you descend to your position of rest, as already described and practised. It is important not to turn or twist the head or body; although we rotate awareness through a full circle, the body and head remain perfectly balanced and relaxed, facing forward.

During this part of the exercise, people sometimes have problems deciding how far their awareness extends. In practice it is best to assume that you are extending your perceptions no further than the length of your outstretched arms; thus by rotation of the Directions as described, you define a sphere of awareness and energy around yourself. There is a wealth of magical and metaphysical potential 'n this part of the exercise; the sphere of consciousness or Being ultimately extends through the universe, which is in itself an infinite sphere of expansion/contraction. For practical purposes, however, we work to more modest personal dimensions, though in developed work the awareness can be focused through the use of the imagination into other dimensions, to distant locations, or to make contact with other entities. We shall leave all of this aside for the present, and remain working with our breath and uttering the Directions.[19]

Once the basic breathing, balancing and orientating exercise has been practised until it is familiar and easy to carry out, we move on to the next stage. Before doing so, the basic breathing and balancing work as described above must be done regularly; as with all meditative or inner

Figure 9

# The Lunar Solar and Stellar Modes

In meditational or magical music, particularly Elemental Chants, energies are aroused, uttered as musical shapes, and then rotated through various cycles of combination. There is no rigid or fixed rule for such combinations, but all derive from the basic concept of modulation or 'ringing changes'. Similar rotations are found in prayer cycles, mantrams, scared dance: they all reflect the reiterations and rotations of the Wheel of Life (see Figures 1 and 2), and such spirals and cycles are found through nature in many manifestations.

The examples given here demonstrate a basic reiteration or modal cycle based upon a simple scale of CDEFGABC, which is the basis of all the musical models in this book. Any other starting mode or set of notes could be used: it is the patterns of reiteration or mirrored changes that are important, and not the actual tones uttered, as these will vary from time to time, place to place, person to person. For practical working, however, it is recommended that one basic set of notes is used throughout, such as the one shown here. Idle experiment and changing of tones usually dissipates energy, and deprives us of the empowering levels of energy that are found by steady repetition and attuning exercises.

| C | F | D | E |
|---|---|---|---|
| F | E | C | D |
| D | C | E | F |
| E | D | F | C |

EARTH MODE

| 1 | 4 | 2 | 3 |
|---|---|---|---|
| 4 | 3 | 1 | 2 |
| 2 | 1 | 3 | 4 |
| 3 | 2 | 4 | 1 |

KEY

| D | G | E | F |
|---|---|---|---|
| G | F | D | E |
| E | D | F | G |
| F | E | G | D |

LUNAR MODE

| E | A | F | G |
|---|---|---|---|
| A | G | E | F |
| F | E | G | A |
| G | F | A | E |

SOLAR MODE

| F | B | G | A |
|---|---|---|---|
| B | A | F | G |
| G | F | A | B |
| A | G | B | F |

STELLAR MODE

| G | C | A | B |
|---|---|---|---|
| C | B | G | A |
| A | G | B | C |
| B | A | C | G |

EARTH MODE 2

disciplines, the exercise should be carried out daily, preferably at the same time of day. Ideal times traditionally for this type of work are dawn (literally) or very late at night, around midnight. This is by no means inflexible, and individuals may find that the middle of the afternoon or sunset are equally empowering. The main point is that the breathing and balancing must be done regularly every day, and that the exercise must be worked through at least seven times in succession to have any long-term effects.

Once a day is the minimum required for this type of training; anything less is pointless and trivializing. A serious student or group would gradually build the exercises until they harmonized with the fourfold pattern known as the Wheel of Life. This conceptual model of relative energies and states (see Figure 1) gives inner balance, though it should never be regarded as an icon or a dogmatic set of rules. If the minimum required work is once a day (at a key time which suits the student best, but always at the same time each day), then the maximum is four times a day, to correspond and harmonize with the Four Elements, the Four Quarters, and the Four Seasons. Thus we might carry out the exercises at Dawn, Noon, Evening, and Dusk.

In many world traditions these are the sacred times for singing specific songs or chants, and for playing specific types of music, or even specific musical instruments. The foundation of this cyclical approach to energies, music, and consciousness is to attune to the natural phases and harmonies of the land and planet, as they are expressed within one's immediate environment.

## Primal Utterances
### (*third month*)

Having built up the power of breath, and developed some degree of skill in orientating to the Four Directions, we now begin to bring in the deeper levels of the training, which involve dedicated and precise use of the imaginative forces. The following stages are added to the physical exercise:

a) Before inhaling and rising on the toes, pause for a moment of stillness. This involves the ancient technique of suspending the activity of the mind, reducing activity as near to Nothing as possible. There are a number of training techniques suitable for this, and one is included at the end of this chapter (see page 155). The first inhaling of breath comes from this state of Peace, of Stillness, and the nearer we can approach to stillness, the more effective the breath, balance, and utterances will be (*third into fourth month*). This part of the training cannot be rushed or passed over, for all that follows simply will not work without it.

b)   The simple exhalation and gentle counting is replaced by utterance of key sounds. These are usually the Elemental vowels, with one vowel attuned to each Direction. (See Chapter 12 for a more detailed description of the use of vowels in association with the Four Elements.)

c)   Thus we breathe in, rise upon the toes, raising arms to a horizontal position. The breath is then exhaled slowly while uttering the four basic vowels in a simple pitched chant, on one single level of pitch or note. The note is, at first, whatever note arises spontaneously from within you. No more is needed in the way of vocalization at this stage, and that spontaneous note, energized breath, and vowels merge together to generate a potent sequence. The Vowels are identified with the Four Directions: Before, Right, Behind, and Left (see Figure 7). (*fourth into fifth months*)

d)   Above, Below, and Within. With sufficient practice, there will be ample breath remaining after uttering four vowels to the four directions to utter three further tones. These are uttered in the following order: Above, directing attention to a point just above the crown of the head; Below, directing attention to the point where the feet contact the earth (or floor if you are in a building, but visualization of contact with the earth below must be clear); Within, focusing upon what is often called the Heart Centre, a power centre or *chakra* approximately in the centre of the physical body. As there are a number of slightly varying teachings concerning Power Centres, we must remain within the framework of this particular tradition, in which the Heart Centre is usually called the Solar Centre: a central locus or harmonic point of balance within each and every one of us. Though we visualize this as having a central physical location, in point of fact it can and does move, both during specific exercises, and during the phases of a lifetime. Such refinements, however, are not directly relevant to our present basic training.

The constituents of empowered voice may be summarized as follows:

## Individual work

1.   Breath and breath control

2.   Utterance of tones, musical shapes, and overtones
3.   Vowel sounds
4.   Energized Names, Words, Calls (addition of consonants)

## Group work
(includes 1–4 above before any group work becomes effective)
5.   Group utterance of tones, shapes, and overtones
6.   Selected harmonic patterns built through group chant/utterance
7.   Call and response

## Further developments of group work
9.   Movement: ranges from simple, relatively static movements (hand movements and steps) to complex dance patterns
10.  Repetition of tone cycles and patterns and attuning of locations through empowered music

Two essential aspects of this work have not been listed separately, as they run through all of the general categories listed above, and through all meditative, visualizing, and magical and spiritual arts.

The first is *controlled use of the imagination*. This may involve telesmatic images (gods, goddesses, saints, angels, and so forth) or carefully defined inner-world locations such as landscapes, Elemental scenarios or symbolic structures such as temples, abbeys, even entire other worlds complete with inhabitants.[19]

The second is *arousal and direction of the vital energies*. This is known in various guises, but essentially involves a response from within oneself which occasions a change of focus and intensity in the centres of vital energy. These are known as Power Centres or *chakras*, while the energy itself is known as *the Inner Fire* or *kundalini*. Various traditions teach refinements of the location and arousal of power centres, and the opening out and harmonic motion of the energies is closely connected to the pitch, shape, and harmonics of empowered chant, vowels utterances, and specific calls or words of power.

The most famous example, perhaps, is the Tibetan Buddhist *Om Mani Padme Hum,* which involves an arousal and circulation of energy not only within the individual or group but through many worlds and dimensions. Other prayers, chants, and patterns of power are found in other religious and magical traditions, for the concept of the highly empowered chant linked to specific tones and words is found all over the world in all periods of history. Many cults or esoteric groups have specific prayers, calls, chants, and formulae of their own.

There has been a tendency to revive this important tradition in a trivial, commercialized manner with modern pseudo-Eastern cults, mainly aimed at selling books and highly modified semi-traditional techniques to Western students. In such cults, key words or *mantrams* and 'secret' phrases play an important part, but mainly to give the members a feeling of security and isolation from society, separating them out from those who are not members. This is a negative aspect of such traditions, showing how they may be abused.

If we examine the positive aspects, we find classical examples in the great world religions, such as *Aum* and *Amen* or *Alleluhiah*. Certain universal utterances are found in all cultures, and relate to the deepest roots of speech and consciousness itself. More specifically, we find that magical traditions, mystery cults, and other initiatory sources of inner transformation employ phrases or musical calls that relate only to their own tradition, though always bridging over into a more universal comprehension. Such words of power, phrases, and musical utterances can be very effective indeed, for they are examples of fine tuning with highly defined purposes, like expert tools or dedicated equipment.[20]

In rare examples, we find complete systems of calls and utterances taught to humanity by entities dwelling in other dimensions. Perhaps the most published and least understood of these is the Enochian system received by the Elizabethan magus Dr John Dee, through the mediumship of the unsavoury and erratic Edward Kelly.[10] Some of the material in our chapters and appendices comes from such an inner-world contact, and methods of working in this manner and establishing inner-world contact are discussed in Chapter 4. This is a venerable tradition involving music and spiritual or magical arts, and must not be confused with idle spiritualism or fashionable 'channelling', both of which work on a less technical and more general or even trivial level of awareness (when they are not frauds or self-delusion).

### The Elemental Patterns

During various workshops and classes, and in correspondence, people have frequently asked, 'Why are those particular patterns used?' for the Four Elemental Calls. There is no answer to this question in terms of reasons or simple logic: those are the calls for the Elements, and they work very powerfully when properly used. In the time-honoured manner of such things, they were communicated in meditation from an inner-world source.

The original communication consisted only of the four number patterns shown in Figure 8, based upon a sequence of 1-2-3-4, a simple enough sequence, yet it is the ancient foundation of the Pythagorean Tetractys, the Kabbalistic Tree of Life, the Signs of the Zodiac, and the Elemental Circle. Traditionally we are taught that these numbers, 1-2-3-4, hold the keys to the universe, if only we can find appropriate combinations of the units themselves. This profound teaching is mirrored today in the researches and results of modern genetics, which holds the key to the secrets of the life patterns of biological entities.

After the simple brief communication of the number patterns, set out as magical squares with no clues as to their purpose or meaning, the rest had to be discovered through meditation and practical work; including the most basic and important information on which pattern attuned to which Element.

The relationship between the calls, their glyphic potential, and the modal cycles through the worlds are all inherent within the basic concept of four reiterated sequences, one for each Element. The esoteric concepts of octaves, harmonics, resonances, and patterns that reach through the Worlds are the foundation of the perennial wisdom tradition; they are not inventions or ramifications. To this extent it should be possible to find other number sequences, form them up as magical squares, and modulate them through the spiral of octaves, dimensions, and consciousness. The important factor must be that they truly cause an Elemental response, as do the Calls used in this method.

There is always the temptation to apply an intellectual theory to such traditions, one's own favourite set of intervals (four semitones or four quarter tones, perhaps), or a number square based upon lengthy work with a computer. I am aware that a great deal of work can still be done with the concept of Elemental rotations and modes, and would be most interested to hear from anyone with a mathematical or other theory as to why the basic patterns originally communicated to me work so effectively. I would also be interested to hear of any other patterns that might fit into this type of Elemental technique. Such patterns, as glyphs and magic squares, abound in early sources of magical and alchemical material, and are by no means rare or unusual. (Anyone wishing to write may do so care of the publisher, or to the box number listed in the Bibliography for Sulis Music.[19] A stamped addressed envelope or international postal coupon would be helpful if you wish a reply.)

The proof is always in practical work: do the calls or musical patterns arouse the Elements, and move them through worlds; do they cause our power centres (*chakras*) to resonate and amplify, rising through a harmonic sequence to expand consciousness? If so, then we should work with such patterns, and apply them for musical empowerment and inner growth or transformation. If not, then they are merely theories on paper, no matter how attractive they might seem or how satisfying they might be as mental exercises. There are some familiar but tantalizing paradoxes in music: any musician or composer will confirm that very simple, sudden inspiration often generates immensely powerful works, while other long-laboured and profound efforts sometimes fail dismally. There is a degree of spontaneity and elusiveness to spiritual and magical arts; they are not designed to be rigidly complete, but to keep leading us into fresh territory, to always be open-ended. In this context it is possible that if we knew a rigid answer to the why and wherefore of the Elemental Calls, they might be valueless.

## Approaching Silence

There is no better way to conclude a practical chapter on musical exercises than to return to Silence. As suggested in the exercises, the approach to Silence eventually becomes a foundation, an essential realignment of consciousness before any truly effective inner work or Elemental Chanting can be done. It can also give startling new perspectives upon music in general: regular meditation upon and dwelling within Silence causes our responses to music, even old familiar favourites, to change. Often we find that Silence liberates us from musical habits, particularly those of negative repetitive or emotional feedback music. This is merely one part of the deep realignment that occurs with regular approach to Silence in meditation.

There are a number of techniques for approaching Silence, used in both Eastern and Western spiritual disciplines or inner training. We shall concentrate upon one closely associated with the Elemental Chant system described in this book. It is based upon the concept of universal and individual spheres of consciousness/energy/entity, and the Six Directions.

1.  Sit in a relaxed upright position (upon a chair or upon the floor if you prefer). For this exercise the hands are usually laid in the lap, palm up, with the thumb-tips touching – some experimentation will find a comfortable balanced location for the hands using this finger position, either with the back of the left hand over the right, or vice versa. The feet may be lightly crossed at the ankles; again right over left or left over right is found through your own intuition and preference, as it varies from individual to individual. If you adopt a floor-sitting posture, the hand position remains the same, but the legs are usually crossed in the meditators' or hunters' squatting posture,

known around the world since ancient times. Complex yoga postures are not necessary, and should not be taken out of their proper spiritual and cultural context.

2.  After a period of steady calming breathing, with eyes closed, a brief visualization and definition of the Six Directions is made, as described earlier (see pages 145–51). This results in a generally attuned or orientated sphere or field of entity and energy: our self located within the room, the land, the planet, the universe, aligned according to the Directions and as balanced as possible.

3.  We now seek to still customary inner activity (having already stilled outer activity). This is undertaken by inwardly reducing your sense of Time, Space, and Energy.

    a)  seek to suspend your sense of the passage of Time
    b)  seek to suspend your sense of Space
    c)  seek to still all Energies within and around you

    This technique acts upon the entire entity, and makes no separation between inner and outer conditions. The usual method is one of drawing inwards: as time is stilled, as space is withdrawn, and as energy ceases to interact, we pass deeper and deeper within, towards our source of being. All that remains is quiet steady breathing, the breath of life itself.

4.  Emerging from Silence involves drawing in a deep breath and exhaling it. This First Breath of air may then be uttered as the Four Vowels, realigning the stilled sphere of being. We may also go no further than drawing the breath and returning to outer consciousness. With practice it is possible to reach through the three phases of Timelessness, Spacelessness, and Poise (stilled Energy) very rapidly.

    To begin with, however, the Approach to Silence requires patience and repeated simple practice. Strenuous effort will produce the opposite results to those required, and trick the mind into many side alleys of trivial interaction. The secret is to approach the stillness, the Silence, that is already within us, deep at the centre of our being. That silence is the state of un-being upon which our being is founded.

    The approach to Silence creates relative conditions of stillness, peace, and poise. If we truly reached Silence we would pass into a state of existence that cannot be apprehended, for we would reach universal poise, perfect stillness. This condition, if such a word may be used, is found in various definitions in the world's mystical and religious teachings. In our present context, however, we merely seek to Approach Silence, and place no mystical or religious system upon this basic technique of realignment.

# Appendix 1:
# Music from the Ancestors

One of the major problems in writing on esoteric subjects, for both author and reader, is that the subject matter is always, without exception, a matter of experience. No mere words will give an experience; the words simply point the way, offering certain potential routes towards experience. Thus mere intellectual expositions and teachings always fall short of poetry or music, story-telling or even a major novel, for the imaginative, artistic dimension generates an inner experience for the reader or listener, which the textbook or practical manual does not.

With music, as discussed throughout this book, there are many other factors present which lead to a totality of experience greater than any intellectual or factual analysis of techniques or structure. The perennial teaching methods for inner transformation are always experiential, and never confined to systematic analytical or simply intellectual communication. The 'complete system' of spiritual or magical growth is an utterly false modern invention, partly deriving from obsessive Victorian egocentric values, and partly the product of commercialization in modern publishing. No one within a spiritual system, except perhaps a raw beginner, will claim completeness or totality; such completeness would be a terrible imprisonment.

In esoteric studies, spiritual training, inner development through meditation and visualization, or magical arts such as ritual pattern-making, the *will to experience* is of immense importance in such matters. Reading, study, and genuine (or spurious) erudition cannot replace actual experience. A writer on esoteric subjects and traditions has to devise methods of communication which he or she hopes will lead the reader to the threshold of experience and, having crossed that threshold, will also give the student some further insights for future development. The actual crossing of the threshold, however, can be done only by the student: the teacher, even if present in person, cannot cross the threshold for the student, nor can he or she throw a student across against their own will. Many people, probably the greater majority who attempt magical or esoteric training, fail at the earliest thresholds, by simply being unwilling (rather than unable) to cross.

There comes a point, therefore, where theoretical discussion, even proven traditional expositions, must give way to purely practical matters. In this book the transition is mainly made through a series of exercises and operational work programmes, in the hope that readers will undertake the skills, disciplines, and experiences offered, and so decide for themselves.

One further element may be added, to give the reader some further insight or inspiration. This takes the form of recollection or retelling of actual personal experiences working within any esoteric system of spiritual development. In many cases, a simple story, retelling events which link closely to the more obscure subjects under discussion, can convey more than reams of intellectual comparison and recapitulation.

In Western esoteric training it has long been customary to encourage students to keep a diary. Indeed, some training programmes insist upon it and will not persist with students unless they have kept a detailed account of their experiences. Such accounts mainly contain ephemeral subjective reactions, many of which may be disposed of, and will eventually be discarded by the intelligent person when he or she reads their own notes in future years. In time, the note-taking ceases and is replaced by a higher function of memory that develops with regular meditation. There would be little point in publishing a magician's or meditator's regular diary, though this type of journalism is indulged in by unscrupulous editors who fasten upon the work of colourful individuals after their death when, conveniently, the material itself is free of copyright.

The only possible value of such anecdotes is that of example; if we feel while reading that others have truly had certain experiences, and that those experiences could indeed be undertaken by ourselves, then the example is perhaps valuable.

Key events arise in very early experience, and often these will attune the pattern of an entire lifetime. The reasons for this initial powerful response, reported by many meditators or visualizers or ritualists, are complex, but may be briefly discussed here in the context of empowering music. Key events or images, such as early meditations, first magical workings, highly energized visualizations (all of which may be undertaken in musical terms, or with musical support, or through chants and calls such as those described in Chapters 12–14) can give sudden liberation. They are the first breaking of the shell of ignorance and habit and conditioning, the shell that we acquire in our life prior to initiation.

Initiation is not a pompous secretive event, but simply a genuine *restart*, a beginning, a first crossing of the threshold towards inner understanding and enlightenment.

The first initiatory experiences often liberate enormous amounts of energy, and frequently put us in touch with contacts and energies from our past lives, bridging these through to our true inner potential. Thus a dramatic exchange of energies occurs, which then very slowly unfolds in 'real' or outer time.

I propose, therefore, to tell briefly of two musically empowering events that I experienced at the outset of my own esoteric training. Such events have a powerful long-term effect upon the individual development, and though they may be noted in temporary diaries, are in themselves, at resonant or harmonic moments in the life cycle, re-accessible, as they occur upon deep levels of consciousness and exist out of serial time. If this statement seems obscure, it will become clarified as you read the examples themselves.

About 20 years ago, in the late 1960s, I was developing the concert psaltery (mainly by trial and error rather than theory or judgement). My earliest experiences with this instrument, which can now be heard on various records, film, and television scores, and on my own specialist recordings, were of the type discussed in our preceding pages. Most specifically I remember two remarkable inner contact experiences: one was concerned with the construction and tuning of the instrument, and a musical/cosmological theory for its playing, and the other was one of those time-jumping experiences so frequent to meditators within the perennial traditions.

The first experience was mostly lost on me, as at that time I had not studied any of the enduring or traditional cosmological and musical teachings. Therefore I simply did the best I could to realize, make real, the intimations that I was receiving. They came from an image or source which we would identify as the god Apollo, though there are many subtleties to the identity of Apollo, as I was to discover later, and he is not limited to the classical Greek form with which the modern reader is most familiar. Curiously, I was to hear the main sequence to which the psaltery is tuned, and which I was told, in my meditations, corresponds to the seven planets, many years later in a piece by the composer John Foulds, whose work was often based upon inner or spiritual traditions.[21]

The second experience was more accessible to me at that time, as I taped it, and still have the tape: a rather noisy mono cassette. Put very simply, I began to improvise upon the 73-stringed (as it was then) psaltery. For a few minutes I merely improvised material that stretched my hands and used the range of the instrument, but this suddenly changed. As I played I seemed to fall through a gateway or hole, yet remain suspended both in my own time and place and in the new location beyond the gateway. I found that I was witnessing a long procession of people winding up a slope towards a flat open-air site. They were men and women, wearing varicoloured clothing, consisting mainly of heavy robes and deep hoods. Up to this point the vision, if it may be correctly called such (remember, I was still playing the instrument, so it occurred with eyes open as the psaltery cannot be played entirely by touch) seemed little more than a well-defined daydream or spontaneous image arising out of the creative act of musical improvisation. But it was to change very rapidly.

As I looked out of my hole or gate into that other place, I realized, intuitively, that I was observing a religious or ritual procession from ancestral times, and that these people were, in fact, my ancestors or predecessors. I also realized that the ceremony was a druidic one, and that these were members of that ancient aristocratic priesthood (which included both men and women as the classical historians tell us) enacting some kind of ceremonial procession. I could see the long line of people winding away over the hill and out of sight, with the leaders gradually approaching my own location.

To my astonishment, one of the priesthood separated himself from the procession and rapidly strode over towards me. He looked me directly in the face and began to communicate with me. I was very surprised and shocked, and his response to my surprise was one of irritation, as if I was wasting valuable time. He immediately stated, in wordless sequences, that he was a direct ancestor, and that furthermore he would begin my essential musical tuition immediately, and that I was to learn the art of ritual music. There was no question of my refusing!

Even as he spoke, he seemed to see the instrument that I was (still) idly fingering in my own world during my vision. The sight of it took him aback, as he had obviously expected something else, perhaps a cithara or harp. There was a moment of confusion, but he then commenced to directly teach me *through my hands* certain musical phrases and rhythms. Like many musicians, I kept a cassette recorder on the table, right next to my psaltery, and this I switched on.

The experience lasted for 20 minutes or so, and there was much of the music that could not be properly expressed either through my lack of skill or the difference in instruments. It is worth stressing that the ancestor, bard or druid, played through my hands directly; he did not teach me musical phrases mentally which I might then translate on to the instrument. I was relatively inexperienced at such matters in those days, and eventually the contact slipped.

One result of this ancestral encounter was that although the druid played directly through my hands, other more subtle matters were also taking place, and in that 20- or 30-minute experience I learned a great deal that remained stored, dormant, so to speak, for many years. Fragments of this subtle teaching became realized through inner disciplines over the years, and I am sure that there is still much remaining to be done with it.

Such experiences, however, must be taken in the context of a tradition of initiatory visions, and not amplified out of context into any ego-inflating declarations of false destiny or identity.

# Appendix 2:
# Synthesizers and Computers

The technology of music has undergone a radical change in the last 20 years, and it seems likely that it will progress at an enormous rate in the early part of the twenty-first century. At present computers and synthesizers often receive an almost religiously fervent enthusiasm, and anyone speaking out against them is regarded as an anti-technocratic heretic. Without either supporting or criticizing the synthesizer and the computer, both of which I use professionally for creative work along with acoustic musical instruments and the voice, I would like to briefly explore some of the parameters of music synthesis in a non-technical manner, in the light of the holistic approach to music that has been defined in this book.

There are two extremely important aspects of music synthesis that set it apart from everything musical that has occurred during human history.

The first is that the sounds emitted are solely and purely artificial and mathematical: they partake of inflexible formulae based upon systems of temperament, on musical compromises devised to assist mainly the keyboard, and now reduced to standard equations for electronic sound synthesis; they bear no relationship to the sounds of nature.

The second is that the computer/synthesizer can, and nowadays often does, produce music in an automatic and, though the term is perhaps incorrect, 'random' manner. This is to say music devoid of consciousness; the synthesizer merely reiterates automatic patterns according to preprogrammed codes. Let us examine this second situation first; it is in many ways inseparable from the first, though initially they might seem to be different topics.

## Music for Everyone?

Many musicians, especially in the experimental art music and pop music fields, have acclaimed the automatic facilities of the synthesizer: it can be used by anyone (we are told) and brings musical potential right into the home. This is, of course, nonsense, as anyone who has worked with electronic music will confirm, for the labour involved in producing even the simplest of sounds is often vastly disproportionate to the quality of the end results. It may indeed be possible to use severely limited musical toys without grief, but even moderately advanced computer synthesizers are highly labour-intensive before a single phrase of adequate music can be coaxed out of them, even if you have imagined, written or created a brilliant idea or musical structure in the first place, and are dying to emit it as audible music set in your chosen instrumentation.

If you assemble a wave form, program certain variants or simply use a preset sound, you can have a range of timbres available to you. The synthesizer will even sequence (remember) your musical phrases, transform them on various instruments, and play them back. It will also randomize notes and note sequences, without any further input from the musician. It is in this palette-like use of the synthesizer that its greatest potential lies, but the musician has to be knowledgeable both in terms of music and computers to use the synthesizers as an organizational tool; for most users it is either a gimmick, an object that appears to do things easily, or an obsessive technical barrier to musical expression.

The potential of this type of computerized system is still expanding, but it seems to me that it holds a number of inherent difficulties, some upon a purely practical level, and others upon an inner or creative level. Let us consider the creative inner level first, though the two interact continually.

It is now possible to generate music with no creative input at all: the synthesizer, when programmed and switched appropriately, will do it all, using simple computerized formulae that reiterate notes and wave forms. This, it may be argued, is a digitization, a reflection, of what happens in nature. Regrettably, it is not, and for two reasons. First, the note patterns produced are not those of nature, as they have none of the organic expansion or variations that occur in any natural system. It is not yet possible to simulate such natural systems with a computer synthesizer; they are of a complexity that simply cannot be handled by our technology. Yet paradoxically they are extremely simple, working according to laws of shape (morphology) and proportion.

If we *synthesize* these laws and their logarithmic spirals, which may be technically possible, we still cannot fill the synthesis with the infinite inner variants that actually occur; to do so, the synthesizer itself would have to be an entire land or planet. This problem is less apparent if you hear a synthesizer for the first time playing what are, supposedly, the sounds of known instruments, but after the initial novelty it is easy to recognize a synthesizer in almost any musical circumstance, though cunning composers or producers know that if you mix the electronics in with acoustic instruments, the organic sound of the acoustic instrumentations tends to fill out the artificiality of the synthesized sound and cheat the listener's ear.

The problem is highlighted, curiously, with percussion, the one area where we might long for a totally accurate beat to be maintained by a machine. Not so. Synthesized percussion is notorious for its inhuman quality, not because we need the errors that a musician might and does make, but because of the minute subtleties and variations that occur even when a drummer is efficiently holding a simple beat. The synthesizer has no consciousness, it exists in an electronic and mathematical pseudo-dimension divorced from the world of human awareness, life rhythms, and music; it cannot attune to biological sound patterns, or to subtleties of natural acoustics, emotional factors, and all the immense incalculable range of interactions that change every single note as it is uttered by the human musician or singer.

Indeed, the synthesizer is based upon the premise that if you can analyse something and reproduce it according to set reductions or formulae, you have reproduced the thing itself. This is certainly false in music, as it is in any organic or holistic aspect of life, energy, and entity.

So the actual tones, pitched sounds, are very far indeed from the tones and timbres that they synthesize. Even if we take sound samples, by which actual acoustic sounds are recorded into the synthesizers and then reproduced digitally across the keyboard to be played, the sample is truly digitized only in a very tiny range, and the rest of the keyboard bears little or no relationship either mathematically or subjectively in listening to the same sound and note range played upon the instrument originally sampled.

This is simply because of the mathematical foundations of synthesis: the developments of scale from sound samples or analogues of sounds are *theoretical*, and diverge rapidly from natural musical sounds.

The reader will have noticed that an exploration of synthesis in relation to creativity leads us back to the very first situation outlined, that of the synthesizer's relationship to musical sounds that occur in nature. This is because the two apparently separate matters, creativity and accuracy of synthesis, are founded upon the same root, the relationship between living entity, consciousness, and music.

It might be suggested that music generated by a computer is not music at all, as it has none of the inherent factors of music within. It is, in fact, a mathematical structure that results in a superficial resemblance to music, but easily recognized as being a synthesis.

## Computers are Here To Stay

I would not wish, despite my reservations, to be thought of as one of those whining people who assert that any technological progress is potentially dehumanizing. Having used computers and synthesizers in writing, composing, and recording, I simply think that we need a far higher level of technology before they truly liberate us. Computers are here to stay, they are making a tremendous impact into the arts of music-making, but the quality, the end result of that impact, is dependent upon humanity. If we simply play around with noises, sequences, and all the obsessive toy factors of computer synthesis, if we cheat the public by earning money for something which, cynically, we merely recorded by letting the machine emit a few patterns on our behalf, if we think that stacks of equipment will give us some musical skill that we lack or help us to avoid the essential disciplines needed in any creative work, then we are fooling ourselves.

More seriously, the computer/synthesizer is eminently suited to further separate us from the real universal world. We do not need to listen to the sounds of nature (for we have them on floppy disc already), we can live within a digital pseudo-world, in increasing fragmentation and isolation. This is entirely a matter of individual intuition, meditation, and willpower.

One remarkable benefit that computer synthesizers give us, which cannot be underestimated, and in my opinion is perhaps the greatest future for computer music, is that they can demonstrate some of the inherent music in energies and patterns that we would not normally hear. Allowing for all of the foregoing problems with synthesis, it is through such computerized means that we can utter the musical patterns inherent in, say, an atomic structure, the most obscure of apparently random sequences in events, and other previously complex subjects that can be simply presented in modern computation. Any pattern may be analysed, stored as data, and represented as music, and in this sense the computer does us a great service, for it proves the inherent musicality of all being. We would perhaps choose to play such music on other, organic, instruments, however, to return its formulae to the universal world.

Where the computer fails is in the creative and natural levels which are dependent upon very complex holisms and entire entities of relationship that extend to a universal scale. Simple music is one such entity.

Where the computer succeeds is in isolating certain very precisely defined areas of data and representing them in alternative expressions or modes and cycles of presentation. We should never confuse the organic, holistic modality of complex energies, such as those of the Elements within us, with limited and rigid computerized patterns.

One interesting possibility is that the computer/synthesizer will free us from the reductive tyranny of the written musical note – and therefore of much of the elitism that has accumulated around composers, conductors, and art music in general. This liberation, however, seems a long way in the future, as at present we are merely replacing one rigid system (the score) with another (the computer program).

# Appendix 3:
# Plato's *Myth of Er*

The translation which follows is based upon that of Thomas Taylor.

I will tell of a brave man, Er the son of Armenius, by descent a Pamphylian; who happened on a time to die in battle. When the dead were on the tenth day carried off, already corrupted, he was taken up and found still fresh; and being carried home, as he was about to be buried on the twelfth day, when laid upon the funeral pile he revived; and being revived he told what he saw in the other world. He said that after his soul left the body it went with many others, and that they came to a certain mysterious place where there were two chasms in the earth, near to each other, and two other openings in the heavens opposite to them. The judges [of the dead] sat between these openings.

And when they gave judgement they commanded the just to go to the right hand and upwards through the heavens, fixing before them symbols of the judgement pronounced; but the unjust they commanded to the left and downwards, and these, likewise, had behind them evidences of all that they had done. But on Er coming before the judges, they said it behoved him to be a messenger to mortal men concerning things in that place, and they commanded him to hear, and to contemplate everything in that place.

And he saw the souls departing through the two openings, some in one through the heavens, and some through one in the earth after they were judged. And through the other two openings he saw, rising through the one in the earth, souls full of squalidness and dust; and through the other he saw souls descending pure from the heavens, and always on their arrival they seemed as if they came from a long journey, and gladly went to rest themselves in the meadow, as if in a public assembly, and saluted one another, such as were acquainted. And those who rose up out of the earth asked the others concerning the things above, and those from the heavens asked them concerning the things below, and so they talked to one another. One type of soul wailing and weeping whilst they called to mind what and how many things they suffered and saw in their journey under earth, for it was a journey of a thousand years, and the others from the heavens explained their enjoyments and visions of immense beauty....

He also added, that every one, after they had been seven days in the meadow, arising thence, it was requisite for them to depart on the eighth day, and arrive at another place on the fourth day after, whence they perceived from above through the whole heaven and earth, a light extended as a pillar, mostly resembling the rainbow, but more splendid and pure; at which they arrived in one day's journey; and they perceived, being in the middle of the light from heaven, that its extremities were fastened to the sky. For this light was the belt of heaven, like the transverse beams of ships, and kept the whole circumference united. To the extremities the distaff of Necessity is fastened, by which all the revolutions of the world were made, and its spindle and point were both of adamant, but its whirl mixed of this and of other things; and that the nature of the whirl was of such kind, as to its figure, as is any one we see here. But you must conceive it, from what he said, to be of such a kind as this: as if in some great hollow whirl, carved throughout, there was such another, but lesser, within it, adapted to it, like casks fitted one within another; and in the same manner a third, and a fourth, and four others, for that the whirls were eight in all, as circles one within another, each having its rim appearing above the next; the whole forming round the spindle the united solidity of one whirl. The spindle was driven through the middle of the eight; and the first and outmost whirl had the widest circumference, the sixth had the next greatest width; the fourth the third width; then the eighth; the seventh; the fifth; and the second. Likewise the circle of the largest is variegated in colour; the seventh is the brightest, and that of the eighth hath its colour from the shining of the seventh; that of the second and fifth resemble each other, but are more yellow than the rest. But the third hath the whitest colour, the fourth is reddish; the second in whiteness surpasses the sixth. The distaff must turn round in a circle with the whole it carries; and whilst the whole is turning round, the seven inner circles are gently turned round in a contrary direction to the whole. Again, the eighth moves the swiftest; and next to it, and equal to one another, the seventh, the sixth, and the fifth; and the third went in a motion which as appeared to them completed its circle in the same way as the fourth, which in swiftness was the third, and the fifth was the second in speed. The distaff was turned round on the knees of Necessity. And on each of its circles there was seated a Siren on the upper side, carried round, and uttering one note in one tone. But that the whole of them, being eight, composed one harmony. There were another three sitting round at equal distances one from another, each on a throne, the daughters of Necessity, the Fates, in white vestments, and having crowns on their heads; Lachesis, and Clotho, and Atropos, singing to the harmony of the Sirens; Lachesis singing the past, Clotho the present, and Atropos the future. And Clotho, at certain intervals, with her right hand laid hold of the spindle, and along with her mother turned about the outer circle. And Atropos, in like manner, turned the inner ones with her left hand. And Lachesis touched both of these, severally, with either hand. Now after the souls arrive here, it is necessary for them to go directly to Lachesis, and then an herald first of all ranges them in order, and afterwards taking the lots, and the models of lives, from the knees of Lachesis, and ascending a lofty tribunal, he says: 'The speech of the virgin Lachesis, the daughter of Necessity. Souls of a day! This is the beginning of another period of men of mortal race. Your destiny shall not be given you by lot, but you should choose it yourselves. He who draws the first, let him first make choice of a life, to which he must of necessity adhere. Virtue is independent, which every one shall partake of, more or less, according as he honours or dishonours her. The cause is in him who makes the choice, and God is blameless!' When he had said these things, he threw on all of them the lots, and each took up the one which fell beside him, but Er was allowed to take none. And when each had taken it, he knew what number he had drawn.

After all the souls had chosen their lives according to the lots that they drew, they all went in order to Lachesis, and she gave to every one the fate that had been chosen by lot, and sent it along with them to be the guardian of their lives, and the accomplisher of what had been chosen. First of all he [the guardian] conducts the soul to Clotho, to ratify under her hand, and by the whirl of the vortex of her spindle, the destiny the soul had chosen by lot. And after being with her the guardian leads the soul back again to the spinning of Atropos, who makes the destinies irreversible. And from hence they proceed directly under the throne of Necessity; and after the others had passed by this throne, Er also passed, and they all of them marched into the plain of Lethe [Forgetfulness] amidst dreadful heat and scorching, for he said that it is void of trees and everything that the earth produces.

Then, when the night came on, they encamped beside the river Amelete [Indifference] whose water no vessel can contain. Of this water all of them must necessarily drink a certain measure, and such of them as are not preserved by prudence drink more than the measure, and he who drinks always forgets everything. But after they were laid down asleep, and it came to midnight, there was thunder, and an earthquake. They were thence of a sudden carried upwards, some one way, and some another, approaching to generation like stars. But Er himself was forbidden to drink of the water. Where, however, and in what manner, he came into his body, he was entirely ignorant; but suddenly waking up in the morning found himself already laid on the funeral pile.

And this fable has been preserved [by tradition] and is not lost, and so may it preserve us if we are persuaded by its wisdom; for thus may we pass over the river Lethe and our souls not be contaminated.

This remarkable myth, preserved by Plato at the closing of his *Republic*, could command an entire book of interpretation and comparison in its own right. The extracts given above contain the main themes and elements of the myth, and omit various details concerning rebirth, transmigration of souls, and moral lessons concerning evil, tyranny, and folly (supported by contemporary political and satirical allusions).

The perceptive reader will soon realize that the structure of Er's experience in the worlds beyond physical death is similar to the model of the Three Worlds: Heavens (stars), Earth (or middle world), and Underworld. The souls of living creatures rotate in an apparently endless cycle between the worlds, according to inevitable judgements passed upon them which lead to their own willing choice of lots for impending future lives.

A number of very detailed and informative esoteric teachings are included in the myth of Er, many of which are still found in the psychology of magical, meditative, and spiritual disciplines to this day. But of direct interest is the description of the structures of the universe.

After a passage through an intermediate after-death state, leading to judgement and a vision of souls descending and ascending, Er travels to 'another place' in which a cosmic overview is gained. First, a rainbow (chromatic) pillar of light is seen, extended through heaven and earth. Upon reaching the middle of that light, they see that its extremities are 'fastened to the sky'. It is the belt of heaven which, like the transverse beam of a ship, keeps the whole circumference united. This pillar or belt of light is the universal beam or axis, often said to be represented by the Milky Way. The cosmology is that of a circle or sphere, with a unifying principle of light tying the universe together, held in balance just as an Ancient Greek ship was held together (and pushed into shape) by its transverse beam.

To the extremities of this beam of light, Er saw fastened the distaff of Arete, Goddess of Necessity. Through this distaff the revolutions of the world (by which is meant both the universal and the planetary world) are generated. Necessity is the ancient Weaver Goddess, whose distaff blends forces into form, and from whose multi-coloured thread the Fates weave the tapestry of time, space, and events. The distaff has points of adamant, we are told, but its *whirl* or *whorl* (the weighted end which gives weight to generate the spin that twines loose wool into thread) is of a mixture of materials, looking 'as to its figure' like a domestic distaff whorl 'as is any one we see here'. This intriguing vision is all the more significant when we remember that spiralling nebulae were not to be seen or represented for thousands of years by physical or materialist sciences.

Up to this stage we have a cosmic pattern: a universal sphere held in balanced tension by a pillar or pivot of chromatic light; with an anthropomorphic vision of the creative and destructive forces, in the shape of a Weaver Goddess spinning thead out of the stuff of cosmic Being.

Next follows a description of the planetary motions and orbits, showing how the planets of our solar system travel within certain patterns relating to the orbits of one another. The image employed is of casks or spheres fitted proportionally within one another, and persisted as series of mathematical or geometrical figures in many variants as philosophers and scientists developed increasingly detailed models of the planetary orbits.

Thus from the universal sphere, we have moved to the specific sphere of the planets in our solar system. The seven inner whirlings of spheres are the orbits of Saturn, Jupiter, Mars, Venus, Mercury, the Sun, and the Moon. The outer varicoloured whirl or sphere is that of the starry universe. It is in this context that we have the famous musical model of the solar system, in which Sirens utter notes for each planetary orbit.

The three Fates, Lachesis, Clotho, and Atropos, the daughters of the Great Goddess, respectively sing (that is utter or emit in resonance and harmony with one another') the past, present, and future. The present, in the shape of Clotho, turns the universal sphere along with her mother using her right hand. This is the eternal present, Being, rotating into increasing manifestation. It shows that Being is ever present, timeless, and that our concept of the present is a transient reflection of an eternal or transcendent truth. The inner planetary spheres or orbits, however, are touched by the left hand of Atropos, singing the future. This counterbalances the universal energy, and generates a difference between present and future within the spheres of manifestation: time is a phenomenon of stellar and planetary forces in polarized patterns. Lachesis, singing the past, touches both outer and inner spheres with both hands, completing the generation or apparent pattern of time.

It is to the goddess of the past that the souls of the dead first come, for it is the energies of their past lives that will mould or impress patterns for their future rebirth. The rest of the myth deals with the soul's progress towards rebirth and the almost inevitable forgetting of the spiritual worlds.

# Appendix 4:
## *Apollo and Orpheus,*
## *Their Myths and Symbols*
## (William King, 1710)

### Of Apollo

Apollo is describ'd as a Youth, without so much as the Down of a Beard upon his Chin, his Hair long, never cut but dishevel'd and as it were flowing with the Wind; he is crown'd with Laurel, his Garments and Sandals shining with Gold; he holds a Bow and Arrows in his right Hand, and a Harp in his Left; sometimes he has a Shield in one Hand, and the Graces in the other; at other times he is cloath'd with a long Robe, and carries a Harp and a Cup of Nectar, the Symbol of his Divinity; he has a threefold Authority; in Heaven he is the Sun, and so bears the Harp, to signify that all things there are full of Harmony: Upon the Earth he is call'd Liber Pater, and carries a Shield, to shew himself the Protector of Mankind, and that he defends all in Health and Safety; in the infernal Regions he is Apollo, and whoever is struck by his Bow and Arrows is immediately sent thither.

When he appears as the Sun, he rides in a Chariot drawn by the four Horses, Pirous, Eous, Ethon and Phlegon: Every Night he goes to rest in the Ocean till the next Morning, when the Hours prepare his Horses to begin their course again, and open the Gates of Day. The Ancients worshipp'd several by the Name of Apollo, of which Tully mentions four; the first and most ancient was the Son of Vulcan, he was the Tutelary God of the Athenians; the second the Son of Corybas, born in Crete, who contended with Jupiter for the Government of that Island; the third was the Son of Jupiter and Latona, who came from amongst the Hyperboreans to Delphos; the fourth was born in Arcadia, and call'd Nomion, because he was their Lawgiver: Herodotus mentions another, the Son of Dionysus and Isis, who were the same with Osiris and Ceres; Latona, one of the eight Egyptian Deities, was his Nurse and Protectress in Plote, or the floating Island, when Typhon fought the

Children of Osiris to destroy them, he was call'd Orus, and was the last of the Egyptian Kings that were worshipp'd for Deities.

But the famous Actions of all the rest were attributed to the Apollo here treated of, who was the Son of Jupiter and Latona, born in Delos, where the Palm-Tree was shewn that she lean'd upon, when she was deliver'd of him upon the Mountain Cynthus near the River Inopus; but against this Opinion the Ephesians represented to the Roman Senate, that he was born with them, and that they could shew the Olive-Tree on which Latona rested in the Pains of her Travails; that the River was called Chencris, and the Forest Ortygia, whither Apollo retir'd from the Wrath of Jupiter when he had slain the Cyclops; others say he was born in the City Tegyra, where he had a famous Oracle, near which was a Mountain call'd Delos, and at his Temple flow'd two Fountains, call'd the Palm and the Olive, admirable for the Sweetness and Abundance of their Waters.

His Mother was Latona, the Daughter of Cæus the Titan and Phœbe, or as others, of Saturn: Beyond the Country of the Celtæ is a great Island in the Ocean not less than Sicily, inhabited by a People call'd the Hyperboreans, it is of a wonderful Temperature and Fertility, where Fruit is produced twice a Year. Here they say Latona was born, who, being extremely beautiful engag'd the Affections of Jupiter, as soon as Juno had found that she was big with Child, he drove her from the Heavens, and commanded the horrible Serpent Pytho, which sprung from the Impurities of the Earth after Deucalion's Flood, to follow her whithersoever she went, and to eat up her Children. Juno likewise caus'd the whole Earth to swear that she would not afford her any Place to bring forth in; at that time the Island Delos, which had been broken from Sicily, lay under Water, and had not taken the Oath, so that Neptune commanded it to rise in the Ægean Sea, and afford a Reception for the distressed Latona, who fled thither in the shape of a Quail from whence that Island had the Apellation of Ortygia, which agrees with the Greek Name of that Bird. Some say this Island was a Sister of Latona's whose Name was Asteria, and being belov'd and courted by Jupiter, was turn'd into this Island; here Latona was deliver'd of Twins; Diana was born first, and immediately as the Midwife assisted her Mother at the Birth of Apollo, soon after he was born he destroyed the Serpent Pytho with his Arrows; but other Authors say he did not do it till he was come of Age, and that after a long and obstinate Fight. Upon this Occasion there arose so great an Opinion of the Sanctity of the Island Delos, that many Ages after, when Xerxes invaded Greece with a thousand Ships, and destroyed all things sacred and prophane, although the Persian Fleet came upon their Coast, they durst not touch any thing belonging to it.

But Latona's Miseries did not cease here; for flying into Lycia with her Twins, she came to the Fountain Mela, and being deny'd the Water of it by the Shepherd Neocles, and the rest of the Clowns giving her opprobrious Language, she turn'd them into Frogs; when her children grew up, Apollo chose Lycia, Diana went into Crete, and Delos was left for the Residence of Latona.

It was in Lycia that Apollo begat a numerous Offspring; amongst the rest he had Elutherus by Æthusa the Daughter of Neptune; by Evadne he had Janus the Prophet, who begat a Race of Soothsayers call'd Janidæ, who divin'd by cutting the Skins of the Sacrifices; by Atria he had Miletus, from whom a City was so call'd; and Oaxus from whom Oaxia, and Arabus who gave the Name to Arabia; Asteria was the Mother of Idmon the Soothsayer, who going with the Argonauts to get the Golden-Fleece, and wandring too far upon the Shore, was kill'd by a wild Boar; Tœnarus the Prophet and Ismenius were his Sons by Melia; Thestor was the Son of Aglaia, and became Father to Chalcas the Soothsayer, much about the same time that Mopsus was born to Apollo by Manto; Chalcas and Mopsus contended for Preference in the Art of Divination, the latter overcame, and the former died for Grief; by Anathrippe he had Chius, who gave his Name to an Island; and by Achachalide he had Delphus, from whom the Place of the famous Oracle was so call'd, not to mention many others to be found amongst the Poets.

But the most famous of his Sons was Æsculapius (of whom hereafter) by the Nymph Coronis: He was so excellently skill'd in Physick, that he was thought to raise many from the Dead, particularly Glaucus the Son of Minos, and Hippolitus the Son of Theseus; upon this Pluto complained to Jupiter, that the Number of the Dead decreased, and that Æsculapius weaken'd the Empire of the Shades below; at which Jupiter was so incens'd that he slew him with his Thunderbolts; and on the other Part Apollo was enraged to that degree, that he slew the Cyclops who had forged them.

Jupiter, as a Punishment for this Insolence, banished him out of Heaven for a time, so that being depriv'd of his Divinity, he underwent a great deal of Misery upon Earth, insomuch that he put himself into the Service of Admetus King of Thessaly, to keep his Sheep for a Livelihood. He fell into a particular Friendship with his Master, who admir'd his Industry, and his extraordinary Wit and Management; during this Retirement he is said to have invented, or rather to have perfected the Lute, which gave ease to his Misfortunes. Whilst he was watching his Cattle there happen'd to him a very odd Accident; Mercury was born in a Morning, the same Day about Noon he had learn'd Musick, and to play on an Instrument that he had made from the Body of a Tortoise, which he found dried upon the Shore, and call'd it the Lyre; in the Evening he came to Apollo, pleas'd him with the new Invention, and found an Opportunity to steal his Cattle from him; Apollo enrag'd, demanded Restitution, not without Threatnings, but soon found himself disarm'd, for the young Thief had got his Bow and Quiver from him, so that he was forc'd to make a Jest of it, and pass it off in Laughter. Here Authors cannot agree, whether the Cattle Apollo had the Care of, were Cows, Mares or Sheep, though the latter is thought most probable, and the Shepherds sacrifice to him as their Protector.

From Thessaly Apollo went to Sparta, where living near the River Eurotas, he became very fond of a pretty ingenious Youth called Hyacinthus; being at play with him, Zephyrus out of Envy, blew the Quoit that Apollo cast against the Head of the Boy, who immediately fell down dead. Apollo, to preserve the Remembrance of him, caus'd his Blood to produce Violets, or rather ting'd those Flowers with it, and made that Colour which was White before, now to become Purple: This Story signifies, that Flowers are blasted and dry with cold Winds, but bud and flourish with the Sun.

From Sparta he fled to Laomedon King of Troy, where, meeting with Neptune in as bad a Condition as himself, having likewise fallen under the Displeasure of Jupiter, they agreed with Laomedon to make Bricks, and build the Walls of Troy; they wrought long for this ungrateful Master, but saw no hopes of the Reward promis'd them for their Labours, whereupon Apollo sent a Pestilence amongst his People, which caus'd a great Destruction.

Apollo was afterwards Assistant to Alcathous in building a Labyrinth, in which was a Stone where he us'd to lay his Lute when he went to work, which retain'd this faculty, that it would send forth melodious Tunes, when struck with any hard Instrument.

Apollo's peculiar Excellencies were the use of the Bow, his Skill in Physick, his Invention of Musick, and the Art of Divination and Prophecy.

The Arrows of Apollo were always fatal; with them he slew Python and Cyclops, and the Giant Titius that would have ravish'd Diana, who after his Death was thrown into Hell, where two Vultures are perpetually gnawing at his Liver. The unfortunate Niobe, Daughter of Tantalus,

Wife to Amphion, felt the dismal Effects of them; for she having bore a great many children, being seven Sons and seven Daughters, was so vain and rash as to prefer her self to Latona; this so enrag'd the two Twins, that Apollo slew the Males with his Arrows, as they were hunting in Cithæron, and Diana shot the Daughters in the Embraces of the Mother: Jupiter, out of Compassion to Niobe, who always continu'd weeping, turn'd her into a Marble that remain'd upon Syphilus, a Mountain in Phrygia.

Apollo's great Understanding how to cure Diseases, consisted in his Knowledge of the Virtue of Herbs and Plants, which he could best learn from his Mother Isis or Ceres, the same with the Earth; Hippocrates ordered his Disciples to swear by Apollo the God of Medicine.

Apollo likewise gloried much in being the Inventor of Musick, found out as a Comfort and Remedy for the Calamites of human Life, being able to excite or allay all the Passions of Mankind, the Muses therefore were under his Protection, he being their President at least, if not their Father; even the Grasshopper, for being a musical Animal, was sacred to him; and therefore he being the Protector of the Athenians and their Country, they wore golden Grasshoppers ty'd up in their long Hair, out of Respect and Honour to him; he was so jealous of any Rival in this Art, that none pretended to be so, without suffering extremely for it.

Midas, King of Phrygia, being constituted Judge between him and Pan, which could make the greatest Harmony with their Instruments, and giving a foolish Sentence against Apollo, had a pair of Ass's Ears clapp'd to his Head immediately.

Linus, the Grandson of Neptune, who excell'd all Mortals in Musick, for daring to sing with Apollo, was put to a Cruel Death by the Victor.

Nor was the Fate of Marsyas the Son of Vagrus less unhappy. He was a young Satyr, who by chance found a Pipe which Minerva had thrown away; for though she had been the Inventor of it, yet seeing her self one Day in a Fountain, she perceiv'd that the blowing of it disfigured her Cheeks and Countenance, the decent Comeliness of which she preferr'd to the Excellency of her Musik. Marsyas, by his Industry, had attain'd to so much skill as to please the Shepherds and Shepherdesses with it; but Apollo coming to Nysa, he was so vain as to dispute with him, who should be thought the greatest Artist, and the Nysians were to be the Judges: At first the Loudness of the Pipe got the Preference of the Softness of the Lute: But at the second Encounter Apollo joining his Voice to the Instrument, soon obtained his merited Applause. Marsyas complained of Injustice, that his Adversary employed two Arts against him instead of one, and that Judgment was to be given only as to the

Excellency of the Instruments; Apollo reply'd, that either both ought to be allow'd the same Privilege, or both should be restrain'd from making use of their Breath or Mouths, and their Hands only should evidence the Excellency of their Skill; this was thought reasonable, and Apollo being permitted to proceed upon the third Contest, was declared Victor, and immediately hung his Adversary up upon the next Pine-Tree, and flayed him alive; afterwards out of Compassion he chang'd him into a River of the same Name, which rises near the Springs of the River Mæander, and passing through the City Cœlena, at last runs into it.

The God Apollo was most famous for Divination and Prophecy, and therefore was had in the greatest Honour amongst all Nations, being instructed in that Art by Pan, the Son of Jupiter, and the Nymph Thymbris; he went to Delphos, where Themis at that time gave her Answers; but when the Serpent Pytho hinder'd him from coming to the Cavern, Apollo slew him, and so possess'd himself of the Oracle. The City Delphos lies in Bœotia, and is suppos'd to be in the middle of the World; for when Jupiter sent forth two Eagles at the same time, one from the East, the other from the West, they both met at that Place exactly, in Memory whereof a Golden Eagle was there deposited.

Here Apollo had the most celebrated and richest Temple in Greece; for all Nations vy'd with one another in sending extraordinary Presents thither. Crœsus, the rich King of Lydia, gave a thousand Ingots of Gold to make an Altar there; and Phalaris, the Tyrant of Agrigentum, made a present of a Brazen Bull, which was a Masterpiece of Art, and a Testimony of his Piety. The Answers which Apollo gave here were suppos'd to be receiv'd by him from Jupiter; they were deliver'd by a Virgin call'd Pythia or Phœbus, who was plac'd upon a Vessel or Stool with three Feet, call'd also Cortina, from the Skin of Python, with which it was cover'd. Opinions differ as to the Manner how this Woman understood the Minds of the Gods. Tully supposes, that some Vapours exhal'd out of the Earth and affected her Brain, and rais'd in it a Power of Divination. Neptune, according to some Authors, was possest of Delphos, and Apollo gave Answers in Calabria, till a mutual Exchange was agreed of between them.

Apollo was worshipp'd with great Veneration by the Falisci, in a Mountain call'd Soracte, where his Priests were of that Sanctity and Purity of Life, that they could walk upon burning Coals without being hurt by them.

The Romans built him many Temples; but Augustus, after the Victory of Actium which he obtain'd over Antony and Cleopatra Queen of Egypt, out of Gratitude to this Deity that he had address'd himself to in the beginning of the Flight, first built him a Chapel upon the Prom-ontory of Actium, and renew'd the solemn Games to him; and then rais'd him as a Temple upon the Mount Palatine in Rome, whose Structure and Magnificence were almost incredible: It was all of Marble from Claros, with divers Materials both within and without, which were much more costly: There was a spacious Portico for the holding a Library of Greek and Latin Authors; in the place before the Temple were four Cows of Brass, representing the Daughters of Prætus King of Argus, who were chang'd into that Shape for contending with Juno for Beauty, done by the Hand of Myron; the Gates were of Ivory, enrich'd with much Carving; in the Frontispiece was the Chariot of the Sun of massy Gold, with Rays of as vigorous Light as the true ones: And within, besides admirable Painting, there was the Statue of the God by the Hand of Scopas, with another Giant-like Figure in Brass being fifty Foot high. In short, there was every thing that became the Gratitude of such an Emperor to such a Deity.

Apollo, as the other Gods, had a great many Titles from various Causes: he was call'd Phœbus, from the Splendor of his Light; and Delius, from making hidden things manifest, or else from the Place of his Birth; and Cynthius, from a Mountain in the same Island; he had the name of Pæan, from striking the Serpent with his Darts, his Mother and the Spectators all the while crying, Io Pæan, Strike Pæan, which they afterwards continu'd in the Songs of Triumph for this Victory, and all others after great Success. As he is the Sun, he is likewise call'd Pæan, from striking the Earth with his Rays.

The Places where he was worshipp'd were many; from all or most of which he was denominated; as Cryse, Tenedos, Cylla, and Claros, a City in the Region of Colophon: He was call'd Albæus, from a City in Lycia: He was worshipped likewise at Miletus, and amongst the Mœonians.

For the Conveniency of himself and his Priests, he deliver'd Oracles at Delos during six Months of the Summer Season, and at Pateria in Lycia during the other half Year; and upon the Removals of the God there were great Solemnities.

He was call'd Nomius and Agræus, from feeding of Cattle; Puctes, because at Cuffs he kill'd one Phorbus, a cruel Robber that hinder'd the Access to his Temple. He was call'd Delphinius, because when Castalius a Cretan carry'd Men into several Colonies, Apollo guided him in the Shape of a Dolphin.

The Tyrians, being besieg'd by Alexander, had bound the Image of Apollo with Chains of Gold; upon the Conquest of the City, the Chains were taken away, and the God was releas'd, whereupon he was call'd Apollo Philaxandrus, the Friend of Alexander.

The Sacrifices he most delighted in were Lambs, Bulls and Oxen, but there were several other things that were consecrated to him; the Cypress Tree came to be so upon this Occasion. Apollo was very much pleas'd with the Forwardness of a Lad, called Cyparissus, who when he had unfortunately killed a Deer that had been brought up with him, and that he therefore loved exceedingly, fell into such a Melancholy, that he incessantly bewailed the Loss; Apollo, to retrieve him, chang'd him into a Cypress-Tree, and according to his Request, made him a Constant Companion of Mourning and Funerals.

The Crow is sacred to him for foretelling the Weather, by a clear or hoarse Voice shewing the different Changes of it. The Swan is likewise endued with Divination, when, foreseeing his Happiness in Death, he dies with Singing and Pleasure. The Wolf is not unacceptable to him, not only because he spar'd his Flocks when he was a Shepherd, but because the Furiousness of Heat is express'd by him, and the Perspicuity and Sharpness of his Eyes are fittest to represent the Foresight of Prophecy. It is remarkable, that most of the things Apollo delighted in, depended upon the Sun, or bore some Resemblance to it; the Palm and Olive Tree, under whose Shelter he was born, always grow in warm Countries, and their Fruit cannot be distant from the Sun; the Laurel Tree is of a hot Nature, always flourishing, and conducing to Divination and Poetick Raptures, and the Leaves of it put under the Pillow, produce true Dreams; the Juniper, whose Branches and Berries were us'd by the Sythians in their Mysteries, is of an extraordinary hot Nature; the Hawk has eyes as fierce as the Sun, the Cock foretells his rising, and the Grasshoppers have their Rise and Subsistance from him; and lastly, the Bull represents him in his full Heat and Fury.

In ancient Times the young Men that nourish'd long Hair, when they began to have Beards, us'd to deposite their Locks as sacred to Apollo in his Temple, and so the Virgins did their Girdles to Diana.

Apollo was often sensible of the Passion of Love, and transform'd himself into various Shapes to accomplish his Amours, as into those of a Stag, a Hawk, and a Lion.

He pass'd some time with Venus in the Island of Rhodes, and during their stay there, it rain'd Gold, and the Earth was clothed with Lillies and Roses, from which last Flower the Island took its Name, or rather from the Nymph Rhodia, who was likewise belov'd by him. He seem'd to delight in that Place more than in any other Part of the Earth, because there is no Day so very dark or cloudy, but that the Sun appears to the

Inhabitants; the Rhodians dedicated to him a Colossus of Brass of eight hundred Feet in height, and of a proportionate Bigness, which was reputed one of the seven Wonders of the World.

He fell in Love with Daphne, who preferr'd a Youth call'd Leucippus before him; Apollo envying his Happiness, inspir'd him with the Thought of putting on the habit of a Virgin, and so accompanying with the Nymphs, they would have him bathe with them in the River Ladon; he obstinately refus'd, and was thereupon discover'd by them, and stabb'd to the Heart with many Daggers; Apollo afterwards pursu'd the Nymph, who, to avoid him, by her Prayers to the Gods, was turn'd into a Laurel.

The Nymph Bolina chose rather to throw her self into the Ocean than upon his Importunities to lose her Virginity, upon which Apollo rendred her immortal; he had the same Passion for Castalia; but she vanish'd into a Fountain. Being enamour'd with Leucothoe the Daughter of Orcamus King of Babylon, he came into her Chamber in the Shape of her Mother Eurynome; her Sister Clytie being jealous, acquainted her Father with it, who was so enrag'd, that he order'd Leucothoe to be buried alive; but Apollo took pity of her, and chang'd her into a Tree that drops Frankincense; for this Fact he utterly deserted Clytie, who pin'd away with her Eyes continually looking up to the Sun, till she was turn'd into a Flower call'd the Heliotrope, that moves itself always on the side he is of, to see him.

They who pretend to turn such Matters to true History tell us, that Apollo was King of the Arcadians, who, for ruling too severely, was depos'd from that Dignity, and forc'd to live a private Life; whereupon he fled to Admetus King of Thessaly, who gave him the Command of the Country lying about the River Amphrysus, and he was no otherwise a Shepherd, than as Kings amongst the Ancients were said to be the Shepherds of their People, and in that state indeed, although he was his Friend, he was inferior to Admetus.

## Of the Offspring of Apollo: Æsculapius, Idmon, Linus, Orpheus

The Offspring of Apollo, besides those spoken of before, were famous for their Wit, Parts, Heat and Vigor; or else illustrious for the several Arts in which their Father was excellent; or remarkable for the Excess of their Amours and Passions.

One of most Note was Æsculapius, the God of Physick, and Son of Apollo by the Nymph Coronis: Her Father, King Phlegyas, not knowing that she had conceived, was carrying her with him into Peloponnesus, when she was brought to Bed at the Confines of the Epidaurians in

Sclavonia, where she expos'd the Infant upon a Mountain, which was afterwards call'd Titthias, from nourishing him; for a She Goat came thither to suckle him, being attended by a Bitch, who is said likewise to have given him Milk, and to have observ'd whither she was going; the Shepherd missing them, and searching about the Pastures, found them and the Child together; there were fiery Rays around the Head of the Boy, which made him think there was something Divine in the Appearance, and divulge the same about the whole Country, and thereupon the People came to this Heaven-born Infant, as thinking him the Son of Apollo, to seek Relief for their Diseases; his first Cures were upon Ascles King of Epidaurus, and Nunes King of Daunia that was troubled with a Soreness in his Eyes. Some say Apollo kill'd his beloved Mistress Coronis, out of Jealousy, occasion'd by the indiscreet prattling of Corvus, or the Raven, upon which he chang'd his white Feathers into black.

Others relate the Story thus; that Coronis being big with Child by Apollo, lay with Ischys the Son of Elatus, upon which Diana slew her to revenge her Brother's Disgrace; but as she was upon the Funeral Pile, Mercury, or rather Phœbus himself, preserv'd the Child out of the Ashes, then gave him to one Trigo to be nurs'd and then delivered him to Chiron, of whom mention has been made before, to be educated. There could be no Master more proper for all Accomplishments; by hunting with Diana in the Woods, he had not only learn'd that Art in Perfection, but likewise the Nature of all Simples, and the Method of applying them; he had so light and exquisite a Hand in the Operations of Chirurgery, that he obtained the Name of Chiron from it; his Skill in Musick and upon the Harp was so great; that he could ease and cure Diseases by his Harmony; and such was his Study of the Celestial Bodies, that he knew what Influences each of them had to co-operate; either in the Destruction or Preservation of Mankind.

Æsculapius by his Wife Epione had two Sons, Marchaone and Podalirius, who went to the Trojan War; he had likewise several Daughters by her, and amongst the rest were Hygiæa and Jaso; his most famous Temple was at Epidaurus, where his Image was of Gold and Ivory made by Thrasymedes the Son of Arignotus, of the Island of Paros, sitting upon a Throne of the same Materials; it was crown'd with Rays, had a knotty Stick in one Hand, and with the other Arm lean'd upon a Serpent, and had a Dog lying at its Feet. Once every five Years in the Spring time, the Epidaurians instituted solemn Games to him, which were celebrated nine Days after the Isthmian, in the Grove that he was born in.

He had several famous Temples at Pergamus, Smyrna and Cyrene, in the Island of Cos, and at Trica; in the Temple of Tetrapolis, a City of the Ionians, there were constantly a great number of Persons labouring under various Diseases, and the Walls were cover'd with painted tables, shewing the Maladies and Names of the Votaries, who had been cur'd by his Assistance; and indeed the same Method was us'd in all his other Temples.

Amongst the Phliasians he had a Statue without a Beard, otherwise he was always described with a very long one; he was attended by a Goat, which was his Nurse, or because that Animal us'd to be sacrific'd to him, as being averse to Health, and labouring under a perpetual Fever; the Dog and Cock were held sacred to him for their Vigilancy, a thing principally requisite to a Physician; the Raven was esteem'd his Bird, for its Eyes and Forecast, for he was skilful in Divination, as well as Medicine; it being necessary for a Physician, not only to consider the former Estate of his Patient's Body, but to consult the Preservation of his Health for the future. The Knottiness of his Staff shews the Intricacy of Medicine: and the Serpent twining about it, is an Emblem of Wisdom, and the usefulness of that Creature in sundry Diseases, or because he us'd to transform himself into that Shape.

Cicero says, that Æsculapius and several other Deities were taken into the Number of the Gods, for the Benefits they had bestow'd upon Mankind; for he distinguishes the Gods into those who always inhabited the heavens, and such as were call'd thither for their Merits, as Hercules, Liber, Æsculapius, Castor and Pollux, and Quirinus.

Æsculapius is accounted one of the Gabiri, or the Potent Gods; Historians say he was an Egyptian, and reign'd in Memphis, and that he was born a thousand Years before the Æsculapius of the Græcians. Cicero reckons several of that Name; the first the Son of Apollo, who was worshipp'd by the Arcadians, and found out the use of the Probe and Bandages for Wounds; the second the Brother of Mercury, who was struck with Thunder, and buried at Cynosura; the third the Son of Arsippus and Arsinoe, who found out the Art of Tooth-drawing and purging, and was buried amongst the Arcadians, where he had a Grove near the River Lusius.

Authors can by no means agree, that Æsculapius was the first Inventor of Physick; some attribute it to Prometheus, others to Chiron, others to Pæon, together with his Sister Eriope; they say likewise, that Chiron was famous for Chirurgery, that Apollo found the best Remedies for the Eye-sight, and that Æsculapius was excellent in that part call'd

Clinica, which teaches how to visit and treat the Sick, when they are confin'd to their Beds.

This is certain, that at first when Men lived temperately, and had small variety of Diet, there were but few sorts of Medicines, so that Plato remarks, that in the Trojan War, the Sons of Æsculapius suffer'd a Woman to give their Patient Euripilus Meal and grated Cheese mix'd together, and Pramnian Wine, which were more likely to inflame his Wound, than any ways to ease it; afterwards Herodicus, a Master of Wrestling, being in an ill state of health, found out certain Rules of Living, and a course of Medicines which he deliver'd down to Posterity; Physick continued in this State till the Peloponnesian Wars, when Hippocrates compos'd his Treatises from the Inscriptions that he found in the several Temples of Æsculapius.

It was long before Physick or Æsculapius came to Rome; but a Plague happening, and the Oracle being consulted, it was answered, that they must fetch the God Æsculapius from Epidaurus; whereupon they sent ten Deputies, the chief of which was Quintus Ogulnius, who arriving at the City, went to pay their Adoration to the Deity, when a huge Serpent came out of a Vault, adjoining to the Image, and passing cross the City, went directly to the Ship that waited for the Romans, and lay down in the Cabin of Ogulnius; they set Sail presently, but making some stay at Antium, the Serpent crawled ashore, and went into a neighbouring Temple dedicated to Æsculapius; some Days after it return'd to the Ship, which set Sail for the River Tiber, and coming over-against Rome, the Serpent quitted the Ship, and retir'd into a little Island, where the Romans took care to build a Temple for it, and then immediately the Plague ceas'd.

Idmon was the Son of Apollo by Asterie, he went along with the Argonauts, being respected by them for his Skill in Soothsaying; but wandering farther than he should have done upon the Shore, he was slain by a wild Boar.

Linus was the Son of Terpsichore and Apollo; his Disciples were Thamyris, Orpheus, and Hercules; he was slain by the latter, for ridiculing him; he was born at Thebes, and was a most excellent Poet; he wrote concerning the Origin of the World, when all things, he says, sprang from the same beginning; he wrote likewise concerning the Courses of the Sun and Moon, and the Generation of Animals.

Orpheus was another Son of Apollo by Calliope, and this Opinion has the best Authority, though that of his being the Son of Oeagrus and Calliope be as generally receiv'd; he was born in Thrace, liv'd near the Mountain Rhodope, at the same time with Hercules, and flourished about a hundred Years before Hercules; he was the first that gave the Greeks any insight into Astrology, which together with Divinity, Musick and Poetry, he had learnt in Egypt; he likewise first shewed them the Rites of Bacchus, which from him were call'd Orphica.

He was a Person of consummate Knowledge in the universal Theology of those times, and the wisest, as well as most diligent Scholar of Linus; he found out Expiations for the greatest Crimes, and Rites to appease the Anger of the most provok'd Deities; nor was he less skilful in the Cure of many Diseases.

He says of himself in his Book of Stones, that he could teach Men to understand what was meant by the flight of Birds, and the different Sounds of their voices, so far as to discover what Jupiter was pleas'd to notify by them; that he could stop the course of flying Dragons, and overcome the Poison of Serpents; nay, that he could discover the hidden Intentions of Mens Minds in several Particulars: No wonder then, if by his Musick, as is commonly reported, he could make Birds and Beasts leave their Prey, Forests and Rocks move, rapid Torrents stand still, and Storms cease, to become his Auditors.

He wrote many Volumes of the mutual Generation of the Elements, of the Force of Love in natural Productions, of the Gyants Wars with Jupiter, of the Rape and Mourning for Proserpine, of the Wandring of Ceres, the Labours of Hercules, the Ceremonies of the Idæi and Corybantes, of Stones, of the mysterious Answers of Oracles, of the Sacrifice of Venus and Minerva, of the Mourning of the Ægyptians for Ósyris, of their Lustrations, Auguries, Aruspices, Interpretation of Dreams, Signs, Prodigies and Expiations for the Dead: Insomuch that many have thought, that he and Amphion were two of the principal Magi amongst the Ægyptians.

He married a beautiful Wife call'd Euridice: Aristeus was desperately in Love with her, and would have ravish'd her; but she, to avoid him, flying through By-Paths, was kill'd by the Sting of a Serpent: Orpheus was so concern'd at his Loss, that he went down into Hell by the way of Tænarus to recover her, and by his Song and Harp so surpriz'd the Infernal Deities, that even the inexorable Pluto and Proserpine could not refrain from Tears, and at last suffer'd him to prevail upon them so far, that Euridice should have leave to return with him to the other World, upon Condition, that he should not look back upon her, 'till she came thither; but he, through the Impatience of Love, could not refrain, and so lost her.

Whilst Orpheus was amongst the Shades, he sang the Praises of all the Gods but Bacchus, which by Forgetfulness he omitted: To revenge this Affront, Bacchus inspir'd the Mœnades his Priestesses with such a Fury, that they tore Orpheus to pieces, and scatter'd his Limbs about the Fields, but they were gather'd together by the Muses, because he had been so wonderfully excellent in his Commendations of Apollo. His Head was cast into the River Hebrus, and, together with his Harp, was carried by the Tides to Lesbos, where it was buried. The Harp having seven Strings, which represented the seven Planets, and had been given him by Apollo, was taken up into Heaven, and grac'd with nine Stars, by the nine Muses. Orpheus himself was metamorphos'd into a Swan.

# Bibliography

The following is only a short list for further reading. Many of the books listed contain extensive bibliographies relevant to music consciousness and energy.

1 Stewart, R. J.: *Music and the Elemental Psyche*. Wellingborough: Aquarian Press. 1986.

2 Scott, Cyril: *Music*. London: Rider. 1958.

3 Berendt, Joachim-Ernst: *The Third Ear*. Shaftesbury: Element. 1987.

4 Rudhyar, Dane: *The Magic of Tone and the Art of Music*. London and Boulder: Shambala. 1982.

5 Stewart, R. J.: *Creation Myth*. Shaftesbury: Element. 1989.

6 Stewart, R. J.: *The Mystic Life of Merlin* and *The Prophetic Vision of Merlin*. Harmondsworth: Penguin. 1986. *Prophecy*. Shaftesbury; Element 1990.

7 Graves, Robert: *The White Goddess*. London: Faber. 1961; *The Greek Myths*. Harmondsworth: Penguin. 1955.

8 Stewart, R. J.: *Robert Kirk, Walker Between Worlds*. Shaftesbury: Element. 1990 (*see also* 5).

9 De Santillana, G. and Von Dechend, H.: *Hamlet's Mill*. New York: Godine. 1977.

10 *The Heptarchia Mystica of John Dee*: ed. Robert Turner. Edinburgh: Magnum Opus Hermetic Sourceworks Series. 1983.

11 Cousto, Hans: *The Octave: The Origin of Harmony*. Life Rhythm. 1988.

12 Stewart, R. J.: *The Merlin Tarot*, book and full-colour deck of cards (illustrated by Miranda Gray). Wellingborough: Aquarian Press. 1988.

13 Chambers, G. B.: *Folksong Plainsong*. London: Merlin Press. 1956.

14 Yates, F.: *The Art of Memory*. London: Routledge and Kegan Paul. 1972.

15 Sheldrake, R.: *The Presence of the Past*. London: Collins. 1989; Steinbrecher, E. C.: *The Inner Guide Meditation*. Wellingborough: Aquarian Press. 1988.

16 Godwin, J.: *Music, Magic and Mysticism*. London: Routledge and Kegan Paul. 1986.

17 Goldschmidt, V.: *Über Harmonie und Komplikation*. Berlin: 1901; Keyte, Geoffrey: *The Healing Crystal*. London: Blandford Press. 1989; Baer, N. and V.: *Windows of Light*, San Francisco: Harper and Row. 1984.

18 Gimbel, Theo: *Healing through Colour* and *Form, Sound Colour and Healing*. Saffron Walden: C. W. Daniel Co. 1980 and 1987; Ngakpa, Chögyam: *Rainbow of Liberated Energy*. Shaftesbury: Element. 1987.

19   Stewart, R. J.: *Living Magical Arts*. Poole: Blandford Press. 1987; *Advanced Magical Arts*. Shaftesbury: Element Books. 1988.

20   Specialist cassette recordings of music, visualizations, and related subjects are available from Sulis Music, BCM 3721, London, WC1N 3XX.

21   MacDonald, M.: *John Foulds and His Music*. New York: PRO/AM Music Resources Inc. 1989.

# Index

Acoustics 11, 12, 68, 80, 164
Africa 21, 25, 42, 129
Alchemy 49, 113
Algorithms 111
Alignments, ancient 114–15
*Alleluhiah*, power of 153
Alphabet(s) 71, 73, 93, 95
America 24, 25
Ancestors 46, 68, 157, 160
Angels 85, 92, 152
Apollo 43, 49, 51–6, 159
Archetypes 33, 42, 45, 76, 101, 104, 107
Argonauts 51
Astrology 29
Astronomy 125
Atlantis 110
Attractors, strange- 110
*Aum*, power of 153
Aura 111, 135
Awareness 18, 19, 23, 35, 43, 50, 59, 65, 67, 76, 81, 82, 84, 88

Ballads 24, 101
Bards 116
Berendt, Ernst Joachim 39
Blavatsky, Helena Petrovna 42
Blues, the 46
Breath 14, 50, 58, 60, 80, 84, 85, 117–18, 122–5, 144–52
Britain 46, 53, 121

Calls, Elemental 8, 10, 49, 89, 107, 117, 123, 141–56
Catharsis, value of 63
Cernunnos 47
*Chakras* 26, 137, 151, 152, 154
Chambers, Fr. G. B. 99
Channelling 41, 42, 43, 66, 153
Chant 7, 14, 33, 80, 83, 84, 89, 117, 122, 123, 124, 128, 130, 131, 135, 145, 151, 152

Chaos 11, 49, 71, 76, 80, 93, 110
Christianity 42, 50, 89, 99, 112
Cithara 52, 160
Citharoedus (Apollo) 52
Clairaudience 65–6
Clairvoyance 65–6
Colour 59, 118, 133–9
Composers 20, 21, 22, 39, 41, 42, 49, 69, 83, 90, 109, 164
Computer 71, 90, 109, 111, 114, 118, 133, 152, 162–6
Concentration 67, 136, 145
Consonants 43, 117, 152
Contemplation 29, 59, 60, 67, 68, 81, 100
Correspondences 111, 135
Cosmogony 128
Cosmology 8, 33, 45, 97, 98, 104, 107, 130
Creation 16, 17, 19, 26, 43, 49, 52, 60, 72, 76, 92, 93, 94, 95, 101, 112, 122, 123
Crossroads, music learned at 46
Crystals 57, 60, 109–16

Dance 24, 27, 45, 46, 47, 50, 52, 71, 73, 76, 152
Dee, Dr John 77, 153
Delphi, oracle of 53
Diaphragm 146
Digitization 163
Dionysus 53
Directions, the Sacred 12, 56, 63, 72, 73, 92, 93, 95, 98, 111

Ear 39, 66, 69, 100, 125, 128, 164
Egypt 138
*Eidolons* 104
Einstein, Albert 119
Electronics 164
Electrons 113
Elements, the Four 23, 25, 62, 77, 84,

88, 97, 107, 122, 128, 135–9, 141–4, 151, 153
Emotion 18, 25, 61–4, 82, 85, 88, 89, 124
Empowerment 7, 8, 14–18, 26, 27, 41, 43, 51, 69, 72, 81, 88, 89, 98, 100, 106, 115, 122, 128, 130, 136, 146, 154
Enlightenment 43, 81, 92, 93, 159
Entertainment 22–3, 24, 25, 44, 99, 123
Eros 73
Eternity 90
Etruscans 53
Europe 24, 25, 46, 53, 72, 83, 112, 123
Evolution 21
Exhalation 117, 151

Fairies, music learned from 46–7
Feedback 82, 83, 84, 146
Ficino, Marcilio 11
Fifths 59, 84, 92, 141, 142, 143, 151
Flageolet 47
Folklore 47
Folksong 99, 123
Folk music 24, 25
Foulds, John 159
Fractal mathematics 109, 110

Genetics 7, 9, 16, 26, 72, 101, 130, 154
Glyph 77, 80, 88, 89, 125, 138, 141, 154
Graves, Robert 53
Greece, Ancient 13, 53, 112, 138
Guitarists 46

Hades 52
Harmonics 13, 15–16, 28, 29, 32, 35, 38, 39, 52, 59, 77, 81, 88, 98, 130, 137, 141, 152, 154
Harmony 9, 14, 26, 28, 32–3, 35, 49, 51, 56, 68–9, 81–5, 99, 100, 101, 115, 128, 130, 142, 146
Harp 56, 57, 59, 160
Healing 53, 64
Health 62–4, 125, 134, 146
Hearing 12, 13, 28, 39, 65–9, 82, 101, 141, 142
*Heptarchia Mystica, De* 77
Hermes 52
Hermetic tradition 13, 49, 134
Hierarchies 35, 38, 39
Holism 9, 26, 65, 66, 84, 88, 111, 112, 131, 135, 145

Holography 9, 16, 38, 101
Homer 46, 53
Hymns 101

Illumination 85
Illusion 20, 83
Imagination 8, 18, 42, 43–5, 68, 72, 82, 83, 89, 90, 100, 101, 104, 119, 126, 127, 145, 147, 152
Imbalance 19, 32, 44, 62, 136
Improvisation 160
India, religious music and dances of 73, 76
Industrialization, effects of 22
Inhaling 150
Initiation 41, 158–9
Inspiration 41–7, 50–3, 77, 81, 100, 122, 155, 158
Intellect 52, 85, 88, 119, 138
Intervals 68, 69, 85, 128, 129, 141, 142, 145, 154
Intuition 10, 81, 100, 135, 145, 165

Jazz 25
Jubilations, natural 123
Jupiter 85, 105, 138

Kabbala 49, 118
Kabbalistic symbolism 92, 95, 97, 137, 154
Kepler, Johannes 11, 85, 113, 125–6
Keyboard 105, 143, 144, 163, 164
Kircher, Athanasius 11
*Kundalini*, power of 152

Liturgies 31
Lure 52, 56
Lysergic acid 8

Macrocosm 13, 79, 97, 118
Magic 44, 71, 72, 73, 76, 118, 125, 130, 154
Magician 27, 106, 116, 123, 158
Mandelbrot set 71
Mantrams 84, 89
Mars 85, 105, 138
Mathematics 8, 11, 32, 45, 49, 72, 77, 104, 109, 111, 119, 125, 128, 130, 134
Mediation 26, 27, 41, 68, 76, 118, 137
Meditation 7, 8, 18, 26, 41, 45, 51, 56, 62, 65–8, 79, 80–2, 85, 88, 98, 100, 107, 110, 125, 135, 136, 145, 153, 154, 157, 158, 165

Mediumship 42, 153
Melody 12, 22, 24, 130
Mercury 85, 105, 138
Merlin 52, 56, 73, 106
Messiaen, Olivier 50
Metaphysics 8, 29, 72, 97, 98, 101, 104, 112, 118, 125, 130
Microcosm 13, 79, 97, 118
Microtonality 68–9, 142, 144
Modes, musical and magical 32, 50, 61, 76, 80, 82, 84, 90, 92, 105, 107, 111, 124, 129, 154
Monotones, synthesized 84
Morphology 163
Movement 11, 42, 50, 61, 62, 65, 67, 73, 76, 85, 114, 136, 152
Musagetes (Apollo) 52
Musicology 27
Mysteries, ancient 51
Mysticism 8, 16, 42, 49, 71, 72, 76, 80, 95, 118
Myth 43, 49, 50–6, 92, 93, 133
*Myth of Er* 53, 92, 133, 167–71

Newton, Isaac 11
Nodes 15, 26, 29, 114, 115, 118, 119, 146
Noise 14, 17, 28, 49, 82, 83, 90, 114
Nuclei 113

Occultism 10, 98, 104
Octave 13, 26, 33, 84, 88, 89, 105, 106, 114, 115, 118, 119, 128, 137, 141–4, 154
Orbits, planetary 9, 34, 85, 112, 113, 125, 130
Orpheus 51–3

Paganism 50
Pan 47, 106
Pantheon 101
Partials 12, 119, 131, 141
Percussion 117, 164
Piping 56
Pitch 13, 86, 100, 135, 136, 141, 143, 152
Plainchant 27, 124
Plainsong 84, 99, 123
Planets 28–9, 32, 34, 49, 59, 68, 72, 80, 85, 88, 98, 104, 105, 111, 112, 113, 119, 125, 133, 138, 159
Platonic solids 101, 125, 137
Plato 33, 82, 93, 130, 167
*Pleroma* 15, 118–19

*Pneuma* 118
Poetry 24, 45, 46, 50, 51, 52, 53, 110, 157
Polarity 13, 49, 79, 105, 106, 138
Pollution 17, 18, 32
Polyphony 68, 85, 128
Prayers 58, 152
Primum Mobile 85, 138
Prophecy 50, 53, 65, 72
Proportion 9, 11, 12, 13, 23, 33, 68, 69, 77, 79, 80, 84, 85, 88, 89, 100, 105, 112, 113, 114, 115, 117, 119, 125, 128, 129, 130, 141, 142, 163
Prostitution, sacred 76
Psaltery 159–60
Psychology 15, 42, 107, 134
Pythagoras 11, 13, 82, 130

Quarter tones 154
Quartz 109, 112, 113, 115

Reels, British and American 25
Relativity 119
Religion 24, 35, 44, 50, 51, 66, 71, 76, 77, 101, 134
*Republic, The* 33, 133
Resonance 12, 17, 23, 29, 32, 33, 52, 53, 58, 62, 64, 68, 72, 79, 81, 93, 95, 113, 115, 122, 128, 137
Rhythm 20, 34, 44, 61, 82, 129, 160
Ritual 65, 72, 73, 76, 100, 123, 157, 160
Rome 112
Rotation 77, 95, 142, 147
Rudhyar, Dane 42

St Cecilia 46
Samples, sound 164
Satie, Eric 135
Saturn 85, 105, 138
Scales 9, 13, 20, 34, 52, 61, 69, 82, 85, 105, 111, 113, 119, 125, 129, 130, 137, 138, 139, 141, 142, 143, 145, 164, 165
Science 9, 13, 15, 28, 44, 47, 64, 72, 104, 112, 125–6
Score, musical 12, 13, 38, 159
Scott, Cyril 20–1
Seasons 22, 34, 63, 115, 138, 150
Seers 27, 116
Seership 65, 72
Semitone 129, 154
*Sepher Yetzirah* 80, 90, 92, 93
Sevenths 129, 142
Sexuality 76

Shaman 27
Shamanistic 123, 131
Sight-reading 39
Sigils 71–3, 77
Silence, power of 11–14, 56–60, 66–8, 84, 88, 155
Singing 56, 121, 124, 130–1, 150
Sinuses 125
Sites, ancient 46, 47, 112–16
Skulls, crystal 112
Song 22, 24, 51, 110, 117, 123, 124, 129
Soul 51, 90, 101
Sound samples 164
Speech 117, 123, 153
Spheres, Music of the 49–50, 51, 66, 68–9, 80, 85, 89, 90, 92–3, 98, 100, 101, 104, 105, 112, 128, 138
Spirit 13, 21, 42, 43, 50, 64, 71, 72, 91, 92, 95, 101, 117, 118, 122, 125, 131
Spiritism 43, 65
Spiritualism 153
Squares, magical and musical 71–3, 77, 154
Steiner, Rudolph 61
Stonehenge 47, 52
Story-telling 99, 157
Stradivarius, violin varnish of 113, 115
Stravinsky, Igor 20
Superstition 9, 16
Symbols 20, 71, 73, 77, 80, 81, 84, 98, 99, 118, 125
Synthesis, sound 134, 162–5
Synthesizers, electronic 69, 161–4

Tantra 76
Tape-recorder (Walkman) 82
Tarot 10, 97–9, 101, 104–8
Telesma 41
*Telesmata* 104
Television 17, 23, 44, 110, 136, 159
Temperament 69, 129, 162
Tempering 69, 144
Temples 27, 28, 29, 32, 42, 43, 53, 72, 112, 124, 152
*Tetractys*, Pythagorean 94, 125, 154
Theosophical Society 20–1, 42, 134
Therapy 45, 53, 61–4, 109, 120, 123, 133

Thirds 39, 59, 66, 67, 68, 85, 91, 95, 100, 104, 105, 129, 137, 142, 143, 147, 150, 151
Thought-forms 62
Throat 125
Timbre 77, 117, 118, 163, 164
Tone 8, 9, 12, 27, 28, 33, 34, 53, 58, 59, 87, 95, 105, 107, 113, 129, 130, 131, 134, 137, 138, 142, 143, 152, 164
Topology 101
Transformation 7, 9, 13, 15, 21, 43, 44, 45, 50, 72, 86, 98, 100, 101, 110, 122, 123, 124, 128, 130, 136, 153, 155, 157
Tuning 69, 107, 153, 159

Ululations, natural 123
Understanding 11, 15, 67, 71, 83, 85, 105, 119, 159
Undertones 69, 119, 151
Underworld 46, 52

Venus 85, 105, 138
Vibration 9, 81, 109, 114, 129, 130, 135
Video 44, 45, 63
Violin 113, 114
Visualization 8, 9, 18, 26, 27, 41, 43, 45, 53, 56, 65, 79, 80, 98, 100, 101, 107, 128, 136, 137, 151, 157
Vitality 53, 77
Vocalization 22, 124, 151
Voice 12, 19, 28, 29, 32, 69, 80, 89, 91, 100, 117–31, 141, 142, 144, 145, 151, 162
Vowels 14, 84, 89, 107, 117, 118, 122, 135, 151, 152

Wisdom 43, 81, 85, 90, 91, 92, 105, 154
Witchcraft 47
Worship 53, 73, 124

Yates, Frances 101
Yoga 146

Zodiac 81, 85, 105, 138, 154
Zones 33, 66, 67, 68, 86, 93, 105, 111, 141